The **MORBID CURIOUS**

The MORBID CURIOUS NO. 3

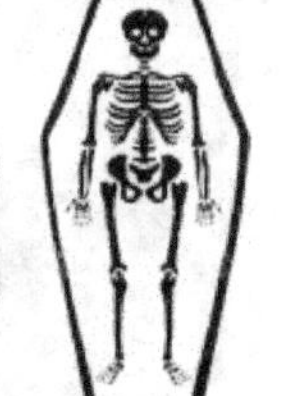

Walpurgisnacht Edition

Welcome back!

We have returned with a new edition of The Morbid Curious for Spring of 2021, which can either be a Walpurgisnacht issue or a Beltane issue, depending on your point of view. You can either celebrate the darkness or the light - it's entirely up to you but I have to say this is another issue that you going to take you down into a dark place. And really, would you want it any other way?

We are back on schedule now after our blood-soaked special edition that we did for Valentine's Day. If that was an issue that you enjoyed, then this one will also be right up your alley. We may have skewing away from mobsters and vengeful lovers this time, but you'll be up to your elbows in ghosts, hauntings, vampires, witches, and anything else that goes bump in the night.

Before you start turning the pages, we want to say THANK YOU! It's been a lot of fun getting to do these journals for you and to be able to offer you tales of ghosts, spirits, true crime, and the unexplained outside of the confines of a book. We have another great collection of writers this time around and a gruesome array of horror that will hopefully keep you turning the pages late into the night! So, thanks again for your support for our little endeavor and we look forward to bringing these journals to you for many years to come!

Troy Taylor
Vernal Equinox 2021

NEW! *In This Edition*

EDITOR AND ART DIRECTOR
Troy Taylor

COVER ART DESIGNER
April Slaughter

CONTACT
ghosts@americanhauntings.net

FRONT COVER
An Uninvited Guest by Adolph von Menzel (1844)

This Book is Published By:
American Hauntings Ink
Jacksonville, Illinois | 217.791.7859
Visit us on the Internet at http://www.americanhauntingsink.com

First Edition - April 2021

Printed in the United States of America

WALPURGISNACHT!
The Most Sinister Night of the Year

That devilish night of fun and frolic was Walpurgisnacht, or the Eve of St. Walpurga, which falls on April 30 each year. According to pagan lore, it is the one night of the year when "evil has full sway over the world."

The dark festival takes its name from St. Walpurga, who is, by the way, the patron saint of rabies. Born in Devon, England, into a local aristocratic family, she was the daughter of Richard the Pilgrim, a lower king of the Saxons, and Wuna of Wessex. She had two brothers, Willibald and Winibald.

In 721, Richard set out on a pilgrimage to Rome with his two sons. Before leaving, he entrusted Walpurga, then 11-years-old, to a convent in Dorset. She had been there only a year before learning that her father had died, and her brothers had become seriously ill in Rome. The young men eventually recovered and Winibald stayed in Rome, while Willibald traveled to the Holy Land.

Walpurga remained at the convent and, in time, became a nun. She remained there until 737, when her uncle, Boniface, recruited his nephews to assist him in converting the pagans of Germany to the Church. Walpurga joined them and became a nun in the double monastery at Heidenheim, which had been founded by her brother, Willibald. He appointed her as his successor and when he died in 751, she was placed in charge.

Walpurga died in 777 - or 779, the records are unclear - and she was buried at Heidenheim, although her remains were moved to Eichstatt a

St. Walpurga - Patron Saint of Rabies and Pagan representation of the Grain Mother

century. She is now considered a patron saint of rabies and a patroness of storms and sailors.

She is also one of the few Catholic saints that was first represented as a pagan figure, possibly thanks to her love for the heathen of Germany. In the earliest depictions of her, she was shown holding two stalks of grain - posing as the pagan Grain Mother. Farmers fashioned replicas of her as corn dolls at harvest time, showing St. Walpurga's blessing of the grain.

Saint Walpurgis Night - or *Sankt Walpurgisnacht* in German - was the name for the eve of her feast day during the Medieval period. The feast day fell on May 1 but is no longer celebrated on that day. But the sinister cousin of the day, April 30, still bears her name.

Though it has never been as culturally popular as Halloween, Walpurgisnacht has managed to cast a shadow over many works of Gothic art, literature, and even music - from the night Bram Stoker chose for Jonathan Harker to meet Count Dracula to Mussorgsky's devilish tune, "Night on Bald Mountain."

But as you might imagine, Walpurgisnacht is much older than any Catholic saint. It was simply another pagan celebration that was "borrowed" by the Church to use for their own

century later. The bones were placed in a rocky niche and then allegedly began to ooze a healing oil that drew pilgrims to her shrine.

She became a saint after the oil exuded from her bones was deemed a credible miracle in the nineteenth

Night on Bald Mountain takes place on Walpurgisnacht and represents the *Brokengespenter* reported on the Brocken in Northern Germany for centuries.

devices. Like Christmas, Easter, and most other religious holidays, it started out as a celebration for another kind of religion entirely.

The origins of Walpurgisnacht stretch back to the pagan celebration of Samhain, or what we call Halloween today. Samhain was the festival that celebrated the start of the darkest months of the year-- winter. That meant that the days grew shorter, food supplies dwindled, and sickness and death lay ahead.

Eventually, though, the season of darkness came to an end, which called for another celebration to be held sis months later called Beltane.

Both festivals were celebrated among the pagan people of Europe for generations - until the Church arrived in the 700s and 800s. Soon, the festivals to Wotan and the rest of the gods, the burning of the dead, and the festivals of the seasons began to be forbidden under penalty of death.

Beltane was eventually replaced by the Feast of St. Walpurga, sort-of the Spring version of All Saint's Day. But just as it was with all the religious days used to replace the pagan festivals, the Feast of St. Walpurga wasn't nearly as interesting to the people as Beltane was. And thanks to this, Walpurgisnacht, the night before the Feast Day, became its own cause for celebration, albeit a much darker one. It began to symbolize the end of a long winter for the people with one last manic embrace of darkness before it was washed away by the light.

And how dark was it? The legends tell some horrific tales. Walpurgisnacht became the largest witch's sabbat of the year, drawing worshippers to isolated spots over the world, where they danced naked around bonfires and had sex with demons. Others claimed they flew on their broomsticks to secret locations where they met with the Devil himself. In Germany, where the celebration began, more of the lore surrounded the tallest mountain in the north part of the country - *Brocken*, the Father of Mountains. The summit of the giant, craggy peak is made up of two formations called the *Hexenaltar* -- Witches' Altar -- and *Teufelskanzel* - the Devil's Pulpit. The mountain is home to dozens of horror stories and even the surrounding plateau has inspired eerie tales. In fact, there are so many that it has become known as *Hexenanzplatz*, the Witches' Dance Floor. It gained the name after a legion of witches took flight to scare away a battalion of Frankish soldiers who tried to invade the area. There are many ancient ruins across the region - like *Heidenwall*, or the Pagan Wall, which offer evidence of the occult activity that had been engrained in the region for centuries.

Goethe, who set the first act of his famous play *Faust* on the *Brocken* during Walpurgisnacht, wasn't the only one inspired by the legends and lore of the celebration.

Anton LaVey was so fascinated by the festival that he established his Church of Satan on April 30, citing Walpurgisnacht as one of the most important holidays of the year.

In contrast, the famous "Night on Bald Mountain" scene in Disney's animated 1940 film *Fantasia* was based on a phenomenon called the *Brokengespenter*, or *Brocken* Specters. They are giant, diffracted shadows created by any person who ventures above the cloud line of the *Brocken*. These massive and startling shadows were dangerous to mountain climbers, especially when mist covered the mountain. Numerous climbers fell to their deaths after encountering them because the shadows made it appear that a giant figure was stalking them. These figures gave rise to the legends of ghosts and demons haunting the *Brocken* - and not just on Walpurgisnacht.

Although it has its roots in history, Walpurgisnacht is still celebrated today in Germany, England, and many other European countries. In America, its embraced by pagans, occult practitioners, and Satanist alike. Many still see it as a sacred holiday and the last night of evil before the months when warmth and light control the world. In many locations, towns are decorated with witch and devil dolls, people dress in costumes, bonfires are lit, a lot of beer is consumed, and costumed revelers celebrate late into the night. Don't miss your chance to pay tribute to this last night of darkness - and lift a glass or two for me while you're at it!

Happy Walpurgisnacht!

20 INNOCENTS

The Horror of the Salem Witch Trials

IN 1692, AN OUTBREAK OF RELIGIOUS MANIA IN THE SMALL MASSACHUSETTS COLONY TOWN OF SALEM CREATED A LEGACY THAT HAS NEVER GONE AWAY. IN THE NIGHTMARE THAT FOLLOWED, 20 INNOCENTS IN THE COMMUNITY WERE PUT TO DEATH AS WITCHES, MAKING SALEM ONE OF THE MOST INFAMOUS PLACES IN AMERICA.

TROY TAYLOR

Historians are often fond of saying that America, during its relatively short history, has been a nation of extremes. It should be no surprise that American religious faiths can also be described in the same way --- extreme.

Our first real taste of American religious mania came from a faith that had been imported to this country and yet made an impact on it that is still being felt today. The Puritans arrived in America in 1620, having fled England because of persecution. They

The Puritans left England to escape religious persecution, only to come to America and persecute those they deemed non-believers here.

wanted a place where they could worship as they saw fit, out from under the thumb of the Church of England. They'd grown disgusted with what they saw as the church's corruption and its abandonment of the purity they demanded from their faith.

As I like to put it, the Puritans left England because of persecution so they could come to America and persecute everyone who didn't believe as they did.

They were an unyielding, humorless people for whom their religious faith dictated all their decisions - personally, in business, and in government. They believed that the Devil influenced anything they disagreed with. Evil lurked everywhere, they believed, and inside of anyone was did not believe the same way they did. Their superstitious fears became the cornerstones of their faith.

The village of Salem was settled in the Massachusetts Colony 1626. Within four years, the Puritans dominated every aspect of its existence. Life there was not easy. Hard work and prayer consumed most of a person's time. There was a genuine fear of insufficient crops and food supplies. There were illnesses and epidemics, Indian attacks, and squabbles and disputes between neighbors. For the religious, they believed the wrath of God was responsible for nearly anything that went wrong, from inclement weather to disease. If the Puritans wanted to improve their fortunes, they believed, they should spend more time being prayerful in the worship of God.

Underlying many of the Puritan's problems was a feeling of helplessness and terror of the unknown. The uneasiness and anxiety of the village created the perfect climate for seeking scapegoats - any affliction could be attributed to the eccentric, the difficult, the elderly, or those not pious enough. It was convenient to accuse them of being witches or sorcerers, in league with the

Devil and his demons, no matter how irrational it seems to us today.

While the adults in Salem faced both genuine and imagined stresses, children were permitted few, if any, of the joys or freedoms associated with childhood. They were to be seen and not heard, to be "obedient, industrious, and prayerful." Boys were taught skills they would need as adults - farming, building, and hunting. They learned to read and write so they could comprehend the Bible. Girls didn't need to be literate. They needed to learn cooking, sewing, and household skills. There was little else to break the grim monotony of their days and nights.

Not surprisingly, the tedious lives of Puritan children created boredom, especially during the long and dreary winter months. In turn, boredom led to mischief and created the witchcraft hysteria of 1692 -- America's first religious mania and one that led to horror and death. It was started by several young girls in Salem whose innocent curiosity in something outside their religious faith spun wildly out of control.

The belief in witches - who carried out the Devil's evil deeds, of course - was as real to the Puritans as the constant threat of the Devil himself. Witchcraft was against the law in most New England colonies and was punishable by death.

And for good reason, it seems.

The Puritans believed that witches could put spells on livestock that made animals become ill or die. Witches even had the power to deform or kill newborn babies. It was the Devil, they believed, not the high infant mortality rates of the era. An inappropriate look, a pointed finger, or harsh word might be construed as an evil curse.

There were other outbreaks of witchcraft in New England in the years before the Devil came to call in Salem Village, but none as famous. Salem was, as one historian put it, a "backwater." It was a small, rural village, with an adult population at the time of only 215 and was plagued by friction and quarrels between various factions, creating enough jealousy, hostility, and religious fervor to make it the perfect place for a witchcraft outbreak.

The events began, ironically, at the home of Reverend Samuel Parris, a relatively inexperienced but pious and strict Puritan minister. In the Parris household lived the reverend, his wife, his nine-year-old daughter, Elizabeth or "Betty," who was a quiet and nervous child, and his 11-year-old niece, Abigail Williams, a bold little girl who dominated her younger cousin. Elizabeth and Abigail were fully committed to the Puritan faith, with its fear of the Devil, demons, and witches. Of the reverend's wife we know little, except that she was a devout woman who spent most of her time doing charitable work in the village. Parris had lived for a time in Barbados and

The Parris home in Salem, where the outbreak of "witchcraft" in the village began.

had brought two black slaves to Salem with him - John Indian, who did outside work, and his wife Tituba, who cooked and cleaned. The children were mostly cared for by Tituba, and with idle time on their hands they were always eager to be entertained with her stories about her island home, culture, and magic. She told fortunes and read palms and showed the girls how to cast harmless spells.

The girls were very proud of this secret knowledge, and they boasted about it to some of their older friends - Mary Walcott, Elizabeth Booth, and Susanna Sheldon - and later, to several others, including Ann Putnam, the malicious daughter of a neurotic, gossipy mother who was largely responsible for the ignorant rumors that later began to spread. Initially, though, the girls all quietly joined Elizabeth and Abigail for stories and demonstrations of fortune-telling. The secret gatherings generated a lot of excitement but also feelings of fear, guilt, and sinfulness in children who had now gone beyond the boundaries of accepted Puritan faith.

The first sign of a serious problem occurred when Elizabeth and Abigail began displaying "peculiar" behavior. They gazed emptily at the ceiling above and seemed to be experiencing strange muscular contractions, twitches, and fits. Reverend Parris and his wife quickly summoned the village doctor for his advice but, not surprisingly since nothing like what we'd consider medicine was being practiced in those days, he had no idea what was wrong with them. His conclusion? "An evil hand is on them," he announced.

To everyone in the village it was clear - the children were victims of witchcraft.

No one knew what to do for the girls except to pray for them. Reverend Parris summoned several other ministers, and they offered sincere and fervent entreaties to God on behalf of the afflicted girls. But Elizabeth and Abigail seemed to worsen. Their bodies became oddly contorted, then stiffened. Their breathing was labored, and they cried loudly, complaining of horrible pains. They suffered fits of dizziness and spells during which they crawled about on all fours and made horrible animal noises. Prayer proved to be of no avail. Accounts stated that the girls screamed as though touched with burning coals whenever sacred words were said over their bodies.

It was clear that they were being bedeviled by witchcraft, but who was working with Satan in Salem Village? Who had bewitched the two girls? Whoever it was, that person had to be found and stopped.

The girls were asked who their tormentors were, but no one could not get a straight answer from either of them. Mary Walcott's aunt, Mary Sibley - described in one account as a "true Puritan busybody" - suspected Tituba and persuaded the slave to make a "witch cake" from an old country recipe, consisting of rye meal and the urine of the afflicted children. The idea was that if the family dog ate the cake made with the urine of the "possessed"

Praying for the afflicted Elizabeth and Abigail, who had been "hexed" by their exposure to witchcraft in Salem.

girls, the dog would begin to act as if it were also bewitched -- if the girls were truly under the influence of witchcraft, that is. When Parris learned of this and accused his daughter of being involved with the making of the cake, she went into such terrible hysterics that he feared she would die.

The girls became increasingly frightened and agitated. They knew they were now in a position where they had to identify someone as a witch. They had no choice - their elders, who could be both intimidating and punishing, insisted on it. So, they accused not one, but three local women as those responsible for their suffering. They named Tituba, Sarah Good, and Sarah Osborne.

Why those three? Anyone who lived in Salem at the time could understand. Tituba was easy to explain. Her stories of the occult and magic had started it all. She was also a woman of color, which made her suspicious in the white, Puritan, backwoods New England community. Sarah Good was a poor, disheveled, homeless woman who roamed the streets begging for shelter for herself and her children. Sarah Osborne's reputation was in question simply because she had stopped attending church.

Warrants were issued for the arrest of the three unfortunate women, and they were ordered to present themselves before two magistrates, John Hathorne and Jonathan Corwin. Allegations were made by Elizabeth and Abigail and - likely because the also wanted attention -- eight other girls who were now "afflicted" by witchcraft. They included the girls who had come to the secret meetings at the Parris home, as well as Ann Putnam, 12, from a well-to-do Salem family; Mercy Lewis, a 17-year-old high-strung Putnam servant; Mary Warren, 20, a servant for the John Proctor family; Elizabeth Booth, 18; Sarah Churchill, a 20-year-old servant for the George Jacobs family; Elizabeth Hubbard, 17, the niece of the doctor's wife; Susannah Shelton, 18; and 17-year-old Mary Walcott, whose father was the parish deacon.

The prisoners were allowed no defense counsel. It was enough for a witness to declare that he had seen the "shape" of the accused riding through the air on a broomstick for his or her word to be believed. It didn't matter how much the poor soul on trial protested the testimony.

During the questioning of the "afflicted," they suddenly fell into convulsions and screamed that they were in pain. They confirmed the accusations that had been made against the accused - their fits and convulsions confirmed it.

When Tituba was questioned, she maintained her innocence at first, then changed her testimony and admitted that she'd had contact with the Devil. Some believe that she was beaten into a confession by Reverend Parris but it's more likely that she was just telling the Puritan judges what they wanted to hear. She confessed to anything she could think of and once started was nearly impossible to stop. She claimed that a "tall man" had come to her and she signed the "Devil's Book." Among the other names listed there were those of Sarah Good and Sarah Osbourne. She had flown to Sabbaths with the Devil, accompanied by a hog, two red cats, and the winged head of a cat that belonged to Sarah Osbourne. Sarah Osborne also had a familiar that was a "yellow dog" and "a thing with a head like a woman, with two legs and wings." Sarah Good had a "yellow bird" that served her as her familiar. There was yet another demonic entity that walked erect, was covered in hair, and was perhaps two or three feet high. There were also "shapes" of red and black that beckoned to her, "Serve me." She claimed that these two shapes had tried to get her to bring them Elizabeth and Abigail, but she had resisted.

The court readily accepted her testimony. It was evident to them that the uneducated slave had been deceived by the Devil and was an innocent victim of the witches. Evidence of this was given as Tituba also became "possessed," rolling her eyes, frothing at the mouth, and screaming that she was being attacked by a demon for having spoken out against the forces of darkness. Her husband also got involved in the ruse and he roared, blasphemed, and threw himself onto the floor of the courtroom, also apparently in agony. The court believed that he, too, was also another victim of the horror that had come to Salem.

Hysteria soon gripped the village. The magistrates had noted that Tituba said nine marks had been made in the Devil's Book. That meant there were still six other witches in the village - who were they?

A dozen people came forward, including some who may have honestly believed what they were saying, claiming that they had seen the "shapes" of others sticking pins into dolls and taking a diabolical sacrament of red-colored bread and wine mixed with blood. Rebecca Nurse, a formerly respected old woman, was dragged from her sickbed to be charged as a witch. A farmer named John Proctor dared to declare that the girls were liars and that their "possession" was self-induced to draw attention to themselves. The result was that he was arrested as a witch and his property was confiscated before he had even been tried.

Women of Salem being brought before their accusers.

Martha Corey angrily denied the rumors that she was a witch and cast doubt on the validity of the any of the accusations that had been made in the village - which eventually sent her to the gallows.

When Martha Corey was accused, villagers were shocked. Unlike the dubious reputations of Sarah Good, Sarah Osborne, and Tituba, Mrs. Corey was an upstanding member of the community and church. But Mrs. Corey had made a serious error in judgment when witch hysteria gripped Salem - skeptical of the claims she neither attended the court appearances of the accused nor did she want her husband, Giles, to attend them. Rumors claimed that she was inclined not to believe in the accusations, and those rumors spread through the village. This started further gossip that suggested Martha Corey was a witch, but for most, this seemed too hard to believe. Before church leaders considered such an allegation, they thought it best to speak with her privately.

The visit went badly. Martha remained skeptical about the goings-on in town and overlooked the fact that those who believed in witchcraft could easily rationalize the idea that even a woman who appeared to be pious could still do the work of the Devil. Martha Corey was arrested on Monday. The previous day she had been in church, disregarding the rumors about her because she was certain of her innocence.

When taken before the magistrates she denied that she had tormented the girls with witchcraft. If she was not responsible, she was asked, who was? She replied, "I do not know. How should I know? I am a gospel woman."

The afflicted girls who were present immediately screamed, "Gospel witch! Gospel witch!" Ann Putnam added that she saw Martha Corey's specter as the other woman invoked the Devil.

Martha was quick to reply, "We must not believe these distracted children!" But the girls showed no signs of calming down. They continued to scream and cry and were convincing enough that Martha joined the other accused in jail.

The hysteria gained strength in the village. Fire and brimstone sermons, the fear of lurking demons, and wild rumors created a troubling atmosphere in the village. This caused even more people to be accused of frolicking with the Devil.

Perhaps the most bizarre -- and certainly most unjust -- arrest for practicing witchcraft was that of Dorcas Good, the five-year-old daughter of Sarah Good. In my opinion, this marks the peak of the collective insanity in Salem. At trial little Dorcas "confessed" that she, like her mother, was a witch. She told the court that her familiar was a snake that sucked out her blood. As "proof" she showed the magistrates a small blister on her hand. That was enough to send her to jail.

Meanwhile, John Proctor's wife, Elizabeth, had also been accused and had joined her husband in jail.

Rebecca Nurse's sister, Sarah Cloyse, was understandably distressed by the accusations made against her sister, knowing they were outrageous and untrue. During a church service she heard Reverend Parris make a biblical reference that was clearly an implication about Rebecca being in league with the Devil. In a fit of anger, she left the meetinghouse, banging the door when she exited so that everyone present heard the noise.

Who would you guess was accused of witchcraft next? If you say Sarah Cloyse, you'd be correct.

In court, Sarah Cloyse stood her ground against her accusers but in the end, her denials gained her nothing in the midst of the hysteria that had gripped the village.

The afflicted girls claimed to have witnessed Sarah's specter, and Tituba's husband, John Indian, alleged that she used sorcery to harm him.

In court, though, Sarah stood her ground. "When did I hurt thee?" she demanded.

"A great many times," he replied.

"Oh, you are a grievous liar," Sarah snapped.

Asked by the judges, the afflicted girls predictably answered that they had witnessed ceremonies in which the Devil gave communion to several witches, including Rebecca and Sarah.

Hearing the accusations, Sarah collapsed. The afflicted girls reacted by mocking her. The meetinghouse burst into a commotion while the girls convulsed into fits and spasms on the floor.

The reaction of the girls was not an isolated incident. Their behavior did everything possible to unsettle the accused. If the prisoner lifted her eyes, the girls all lifted theirs; if she rubbed her face, the girls did the same; if she coughed, the girls all coughed, and so on. If the prisoner denied the charges brought against her, the girls went into a frenzy, howling and throwing themselves on the floor. Still worse, they became the jury and executioner of the accused. One by one the girls were carried to the prisoner and she was forced to take each of their hands. If an afflicted girl continued to rave and thrash about the accused was innocent, but if she became quiet it was assumed that the accused had removed the demon that had been sent to torture her and so was obviously guilty.

The girls had a terrifying effect on not only the trials but on the people of the village, as well. They were constantly seeing "shapes" all over the place, and so unshakable had the belief in them become that at the girl's direction the villagers stabbed at the empty air with swords and pitchforks where the "shapes" were supposed to be.

People in Salem who feared being accused or "cried out," as it was called, began to leave the village. Among them was John Willard, the deputy constable, who had arrested several of the accused witches. In a sudden fit of disgust, he turned on the afflicted girls, accused them of being frauds, and said that they should be hanged for what they had done. The girls retaliated against him by claiming that they had seen his "shape" strangling his nephew, a young man who had recently died. Willard tried to flee but was captured and chained up in prison, accused of having witched to death not only his nephew, several other people, too.

Around this time the afflicted girls decided to announce the identity of another prominent witch -- The Reverend George Burroughs, who had been a minister in Salem several years before. Even though they were shocked at the idea that a minister would be involved, the magistrates quickly dispatched officers to the parish where Burroughs now lived. They stormed into his home in the middle of a meal and dragged him back to Salem. To Burroughs' amazement, he was accused of murdering several soldiers who had been killed near his parish while fighting Indians -- not physically, of course, but as a sinister "shape," just like the other alleged witches. Interestingly, Burroughs' time in Salem had been unpleasant. He'd had a history of disagreements with many people, but especially with the Putnam family. There was quite a bit of animosity between the reverend and Ann's parents, which undoubtedly played a large part in the accusations against him.

More arrests were made on charges of witchcraft -- Bridget Bishop, Abigail Hobbs, Martha Corey's 80-year-old husband, Giles, and John Proctor's servant, Mary Warren, herself one of the afflicted girls. There were questions about Mary's arrest -- she had been an accuser, why was she now being charged? Likely she was badly shaken by the arrest of the Proctors for whom she'd worked. Her behavior became erratic, and she was now confused about the things she'd done as a "victim." When the other tormented girls got wind of Mary's doubts, they quickly tried to quiet her loose talk by claiming that she had bewitched them and has signed the Devil's Book.

When she was brought into court it only took a glance from her to cause the other girls to fall into another round of fits and screams. Mary became emotionally overwhelmed - and it wasn't an act. She was genuinely terrified and became so hysterical that she was removed from court and taken to jail. Several weeks later she admitted to being a witch but blamed John and Elizabeth Proctor - along with others - for her misfortunes. By confessing Mary probably saved her own life. She was freed and again considered one of the afflicted. Typically, those who confessed to being witches were spared

The "afflicted girls" had great power in the community, settling old family quarrels, targeting people who were unliked, and, in the case of Mary Warren, quieting the accusers among them who had started to doubt what they were doing.

the gallows. Those who maintained their innocence were invariably convicted and condemned to hang.

When Bridget Bishop, Abigail Hobbs, and Giles Corey were questioned, both Bishop and Corey insisted that they were not guilty of witchcraft. But their pleas were in vain - as soon as the afflicted girls looked at them the girls fell into outbursts of fits and contortions.

Abigail Hobbs, however, confessed to everything, telling the magistrates that she had "sold herself body and soul to the old boy." She said that's he practiced witchcraft, attending meetings of sorcerers, and drank "red wine with red bread." She was jailed along with the others, but during her confession she implicated nine more people. Arrest warrants were issued for Abigail's parents --

William and Deliverance Hobbs -- Susanna Martin, and Mary Esty, the sister of Rebecca Nurse and Sarah Cloyse.

Shaken by her arrest and the questioning that followed, Deliverance Hobbs began to question her own sanity -- could she be a witch and not know it? Rattled and overwhelmed, she confessed to practicing witchcraft and offered the names of other witches in the village. Her husband William, outraged by the spectacle, insisted that he was innocent of all charges, which, of course, landed him in jail.

Mary Esty, when questioned, kept control of her emotions but was also jailed. Susanna Martin, on the other hand, didn't take the courtroom proceedings seriously at all and even laughed at one point. She doubted the afflicted girls and called them liars. As she was being taken away to jail, she remarked, "A false tongue will never make a guilty person."

When a short time later Mary Esty was released from the jail, her manner so impressed officials that they began to believe she was not guilty. But her freedom didn't last long. Whether genuinely fearful or just malicious, the afflicted girls grew hysterical, especially Mercy Lewis, whose fits frightened everyone who witnessed them. When she cried out Mary's name, the poor woman was placed back behind bars.

Meanwhile, a new governor had arrived from England, Sir William Phips, and he came to the village with Increase Mather, the father of Cotton Mather, and later president of Harvard University. Mather had been prominent in earlier witch trials in Boston, but Phips was only interested in getting together a military expedition against the French in Canada. He wanted nothing to do with what was going on in Salem Village.

After decreeing that all of those who had been accused of witchcraft be kept chained in their cells, he left the business of trying them to the courts. A special court was formed with Deputy Governor William Stoughton as president and six other judges. Whether intentional or not, the fact that judges from a higher court came to Salem elevated the controversy to a new level. This was no longer a matter of village business. The mania became news that gripped the entire Massachusetts colony. The accused were no longer merely being questioned -- they were now going on trial.

Bridget Bishop was the first to be brought before the judges. Her position in the community had contributed to her dilemma. She was twice widowed and was the successful proprietor of a local inn. She also stood out in the community for her wearing of "brightly colored" clothes, which was abhorred by the Puritans who traditionally wore dark, modest clothing. She didn't help her case by appearing in court wearing a "lace-trimmed scarlet bodice." When women assigned by the court examined Bridget's body, they found an "excrescence of flesh," believed to be an extra nipple used by the witch's familiar to feed from her breast. She also didn't help herself by stating that she was innocent. Bridget was pronounced guilty and hanged on Gallows Hill on June 10.

Religious hysteria peaked during the trials when the judges began allowing "spectral evidence" to be admitted in court. This evidence claimed that specters or apparitions of witches tormented and inflicted pain on the innocent. But the specters could only be seen by those who were bewitched. These claims -- along with unsupported claims and hearsay -- were allowed by the Salem judges. This seems mind-boggling to us today, but in the religious climate of New England in the seventeenth century it seemed perfectly reasonable.

In late June, the fates of Sarah Good, Elizabeth Howe, Susanna Martin, Sarah Wilds, and Rebecca Nurse were also sealed. Four of them were found guilty and sentenced to hang. Only Rebecca Nurse had been found not guilty. Her good reputation served her well - at first. Her numerous friends and family were brave enough to

There would be 19 innocents hanged in Salem during the witch trials - the last to die would be crushed to death by rocks.

testify on her behalf and she was found to be not guilty of the crimes for which she was accused. Instantly the courtroom was plunged into chaos. The afflicted girls howled, pulled their hair, and rolled around on the floor, screaming that the woman was guilty. Unbelievably, she was brought back into court and the jury was ordered to think things over again. This time they reversed their verdict, and she was found guilty. On Tuesday, July 19, she and the other four women hanged as witches in Salem.

Sarah Good's last words proclaimed her innocence, and as the noose was placed around her neck, she rebuked the Reverend Nicholas Noyes, who stood nearby and had accused her of being a witch. "You are a liar," she shouted. "I am no more a witch than you are a wizard, and if you take away my life, God will give you blood to drink."

Eerily Sarah's prediction came true. Years later Noyes choked to death on his own blood following a throat hemorrhage.

The terror continued to spread. Scores of people were "cried out," and the court continued its travesty of justice. Prisoners who confessed could hope for clemency, but those who denied their guilt were condemned.

In July, John Proctor, still in the dismal confines of the jail, wrote to Boston ministers to plead that the witch trials be held in Boston with new judges on the bench. He was certain that the "witch hunts" were based largely on lies and intimidation. But his letters had little effect. In early August, he and his wife, Elizabeth, stood trial, as did Reverend George Burroughs, and three others. More than 30 people from Ipswich, Massachusetts, where John Proctor once lived, appealed to the judges on his behalf, hoping to save his life. Nearly two dozen neighbors from Salem also offered support. But their efforts were in vain -- John and Elizabeth were declared guilty, along with the others. Only Elizabeth was spared from being hanged. She was pregnant at the time and under Puritan law the killing of her innocent, unborn child was forbidden.

George Jacobs was convicted on the word of his granddaughter, Margaret. When she had been arrested on witchcraft charges, she had offered his name because she feared being tortured and hanged. Although she later stated in court that her confession had been coerced and that her testimony had been "false and untrue," it had no effect on the fate of her grandfather, who was condemned to die on the gallows.

The trials and executions continued. In September, 15 more people were sentenced to death. On just one day, September 22, eight were hanged, including Martha Corey. Several of the convicted pleaded to the governor, judges, and clergy for clemency, but their appeals fell on deaf ears.

Giles Corey, Martha's husband, had also been accused of practicing witchcraft. Although the old man knew he was not guilty, he also understood that if he claimed to be innocent, he'd be convicted anyway. A proud man, he refused to falsely plead guilty just to save his life and satisfy his accusers. So, Corey refused to enter a plea at all. In fact, he did not utter a single word in court. Therefore, under Puritan law, he could not be brought to trial.

But he paid the price for his bold silence.

He was brutally punished, and the court made no allowance for Giles's advanced age. He was laid on the ground while heavy stones were placed on him until he was crushed to death under their weight. He lasted for two days of suffering before he finally died.

His courage deeply affected the people of the village, as did his composure and refusal to lie.

The seeds of doubt had finally been sown in Salem Village.

Following the death sentences of September, the court recessed with plans to reconvene later in the fall -- but it never happened. There was a marked shift in the attitude of the villagers about the trials. People were beginning to speak out. Cotton Mather issued a warning about depending on "spectral evidence." An influential Boston merchant named Thomas Brattle wrote a letter in which he objected to the way that the Salem trials had been conducted. A magistrate from Salisbury, Robert Pike, wrote that he was skeptical of both what the afflicted girls claimed, and the of types of highly questionable evidence permitted to convict someone of witchcraft. He did not doubt the reality of witches, he stated, but suggested the Devil was doing his nefarious work through the afflicted, not the witches. Because of this innocent people were being accused in some instances because the Devil was commanding the afflicted to falsely blame the righteous.

But it was Governor Phips who finally put the whole thing to an end. He returned from the Canadian border and was shocked to find that more than 150 people were still chained up in jail, waiting to be put on trial for witchcraft. He was dismayed that his

Giles Corey - who had already witnessed his wife hanged as a witch - was the oldest of the defendants brought to trial. He refused to speak in court was pressed to death by heavy stones.

(Below) His burial site today is - ironically - marked by this large rock.

special court had not found a solution to the problem. It seemed to have made things worse. In October he ordered that no one else would be jailed, except in extreme cases. He also decreed that, in the future, "spectral evidence" would be inadmissible in his courts. This made

trying the other defendants nearly impossible, but laws had to be followed. Those that remained in jail finally had their day in court in January 1693. There were 52 people brought to trial, and three were convicted who confessed to witchcraft. All but those three were set free -- those that confessed were sentenced to hang. But the royal attorney general ruled the evidence against the condemned was insufficient and Governor Phips commuted their sentences.

The Salem witch hysteria finally came to an end.

By the spring of 1693, the witch hunts were over, but the acrimony that they created between villagers would linger for years. The accusations, harsh words, and bitter memories created permanent rifts between former friends and neighbors. Many of those who fled Salem during the hysteria chose to never return.

Once public sentiment shifted away from the "afflicted girls," they withdrew from sight. Only Ann Putnam publicly admitted the wrongdoing that she'd taken part in. In 1706, she requested to be allowed back as a member of the church in Salem Village, and Reverend Green read her apology from the pulpit. In the spirit of healing, she was forgiven and allowed to return to the church.

But not all were forgiven. Many were angry with Reverend Parris for his rush in demanding that the children accuse others of supposedly bewitching them. The most furious were, of course, the relatives of those jailed, tortured, and executed. Parris was forced to leave Salem in 1697 and he never returned.

Eventually, most people came to realize that the Salem insanity was a deception instigated by fear and religious extremism. Throughout the Massachusetts colony, the date January 4, 1797 was set aside as a day of fasting and prayer to ask "God's forgiveness" for the tragedy of the witch trials. One of the judges, Samuel Sewall, wrote a letter that his minister read to the congregation. Sewall acknowledged his terrible mistake when he condemned innocent people to death. All he could do now, he wrote, was plead for absolution from God and his fellow men and women. Also, on that same day, former trial jurors admitted their mistakes, especially in believing that "spectral evidence" was sufficient to send someone to the gallows. They begged for forgiveness and deeply apologized, saying they'd fall under the power of a strong "delusion."

But no number of apologies could erase the damage that had been done.

A view of the Old Burying Ground in Salem today. In these modern times, the village embraces its heritage of the witch trials, becoming a haven for real-life witches and a very different place from what it was three centuries ago.

In all, 20 people went to their deaths -- 19 of them hanged and one crushed. Dozens of others had been jailed. Of those accused, 50 confessed to being witches, likely under the threat of torture. Several died in jail, undoubtedly from the deplorable conditions.

And then there was little Dorcas Good, the five-year-old sent to jail as a witch. She nearly went insane from her experiences and remained traumatized for the rest of her life.

An apology, no matter how sincere, was an inadequate gesture considering the horror that occurred.

What happened in that small New England village? Experts have blamed fraud, class conflict, village factions fighting one another, sexual repression, accidental poisoning, hysteria, actual witchcraft, and, of course, religious extremism. Likely no one explanation will suffice. It was probably a combination of several things, but there is no doubt that the extreme faith of the Puritans was a strong factor. If not for their willingness to blame the Devil for every illness, crop failure, and storm that occurred in and around the village, the witch hunts would never have occurred at all.

The region teetered on the edge of madness and changed the way that Americans thought about religion for years to come. The reaction that so many people had to the rigid dogma of the Puritans, combined with a coming era of "enlightened" thinking, left little room for religious mania in the eighteenth century.

America's Puritan heritage cast a shadow over the history of the country, and it influenced many opinions and fears about religion for more than a century.

The Eternal Lives of the
LADIES OF THE NIGHT

Amanda R. Woomer
Spook Eats

Prostitution: it's as old as humanity itself and dubbed "the world's oldest profession." Over the centuries, some women have turned to it out of desperation, while others managed to create a lucrative business from it. To some, it was shameful. To others, it was stability. Despite the stigma that sex work still experiences, historians are beginning to look at prostitutes, brothels, and the subculture these environments created in the paranormal world and the mundane.

Usually associated with dance halls and saloons, brothels were built to house both the working girls and the business itself (traditionally run by a woman or Madam). Just like bars and hotels of the 21st Century, these brothels, bordellos, dance halls, and saloons were liminal spaces where people could constantly come and go seemingly undetected and could be who they wanted to be, even if it was only for one night.

The idea of the bordello nestled above a noisy dance hall with its honky-tonk music playing, saloon girls dancing, and cowboys gambling has left an almost romanticized image in our minds when we think of prostitutes in America. And if we don't think of red garters and feathers nestled in a head of tangled curls, then we

Women in an early San Francisco bordello circa 1890

think of the darker side of these seedy locales: sex, drugs, abortion, alcohol, suicide, and murder. Of course, we shouldn't view history with rose-tinted glasses, nor should we paint everything with such a broad "doom and gloom" brush. Surely there must be a balance when it comes to any aspect of history... even the macabre history of prostitutes in America.

It may come as a shock to some that, in many cases, working in a brothel was a viable job for women (especially women on the frontier). They were provided with shelter in the form of their "cribs," food and drink, and in many cases, burly men would act as security (not much different from our bouncers we see today). Of course, many of these luxuries came at a price: most of their earnings would go towards paying the Madam and the security guard, but life in a brothel was ideal compared to working on the streets.

Despite the impact that brothels had in forming towns and cities all across America, many of these ladies remain nameless blips in history, usually reserved for local legends...

Prostitution district -- Oshiwora, the "Whitechapel" of Dawson in Yukon Territory, 1899 - Photo by Eric A Hegg

some only lucky enough to be remembered as a ghostly Lady in Red.

These women, their customers, the events (both good and bad), and emotions have left an imprint on the buildings they once called home. Luckily for the curious visitor, many of these antiquated buildings are still standing today and survive in the form of restaurants, bars, and hotels. And with diners and travelers coming to visit, these ladies' stories are being told and retold, breathing new life into those who would merely be a nameless woman lying on a bed, paid to look pretty and show a man a good time.

The Red Onion Saloon of Skagway, Alaska, is perhaps one of the finest examples of a business that has embraced its history and the bordello that is still on site. They have transformed the ten rooms where the ladies once worked into a museum. They offer "quickie" tours. Their tour guides are dressed in period clothes. Cori, the museum's curator, shares the true history of working women in Skagway (and it's not nearly as bleak as the history books would have you believe). And most importantly, they share the story of Lydia.

Like most working girls of the 19th Century, no one knows precisely who Lydia was in life, what she looked like, or where she came from. However, they believe she worked in the brothel at some point in its history, contracted syphilis, and hanged herself. Despite this tragic end to her life, it seems this is where Lydia's story only just began.

Over the years, the staff at the museum have come to know Lydia by name. She is such an integral part of the space that if the staff forget to say hello or go too long without acknowledging her, she causes a bit of mischief to be noticed. Nearly every day, the tour guides will say Lydia's name and share her story... she has found immortality in death.

And Lydia isn't the only lady of the night experiencing eternal life even after her death.

Nina (pronounced Nigh-na) is said to haunt Old Town Pizza and Brewing in Portland, Oregon. What is now one of the city's hippest pizza joints was once the Merchant Hotel. Built at the end of the 19th Century, it was part of Old North End, the dodgy part of town, and built on top of Portland's infamous Shanghai Tunnels. Prostitution was offered at the hotel, and many believe Nina was one of the girls sold into the sex trade. According to Nina's tragic tale, a group of traveling missionaries offered her freedom in exchange for information on the Merchant Hotel's sex trade. Nina agreed to help them, but before she could be saved, she was thrown down an elevator shaft to her death... and that former elevator shaft is now a dining booth you can sit in.

Nina has been known to wander through the restaurant and taproom in the hotel's lobby. Usually seen in a black dress, she walks among diners, watching them as they eat a slice of Ghost Pie (their signature pizza created in her honor).

And it isn't just the "working girls" who have been immortalized thanks to their restless spirits–even the Madams are finding new life in the afterlife.

One Madam remembered even a century after her untimely death is Lucinda Talley, known to run a tight ship at the Peerless Saloon in Anniston, Alabama. One of the finest drinking establishments at the time (no doubt, peerless) as well as one of the first brothels in town, the entire second floor of the Peerless Saloon was the home to five clean rooms for girls to entertain their clients in privacy. At the top of the stairs sat Lucinda Talley, Madam of the Peerless Saloon's brothel, known to carry a gun as she screened potential customers. Lucinda met her end in 1919 when she was accidentally shot by a police officer pursuing a suspect taking refuge in the bordello.

Today, the former brothel is now a banquet hall in the Peerless Saloon. Four fireplaces dot the walls, revealing where four of the private rooms once stood. But they're not the only remnant leftover from its days as a brothel... many believe Lucinda lingers as well, keeping an eye on the business she gave her life for.

To some, a haunting could be seen as a tragic end to a sad life—being

The former elevator shaft where Nina met her grisly end.

Photo courtesy of Old Town Pizza & Brewing

trapped in a dusty old place, doomed to live out eternity unseen and unheard. But many of these women–working girls and Madams, alike–lived life unseen and unheard... each of them was just one of the countless women trying to survive and make a living in a man's world.

And while some found success and fortune in life, many have seen far greater fame in death. Many of these establishments embrace their history and hauntings, protecting the femme phantoms that roam the halls and former cribs. They call out these women's names with affection and respect. They tell their stories... and with each retelling, the lives of Lydia, Nina, and Lucinda -- and so many others -- continue to endure.

THE VIGILANTE MASACRE

The Mysterious Murders of the "Black" Donnelliss

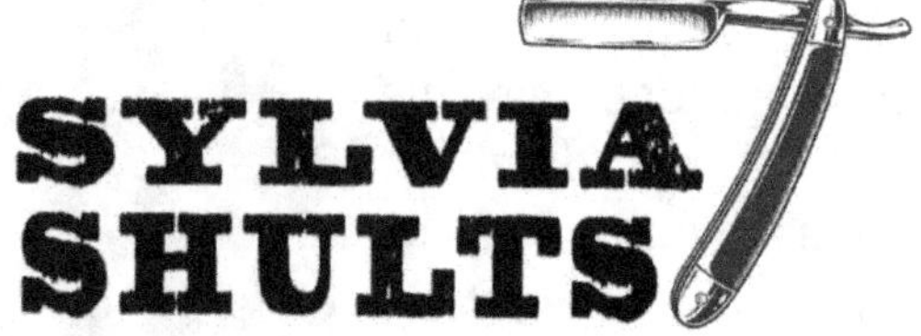

SYLVIA SHULTS

In the 1840s, many immigrants from Ireland showed up on the shores of the New World, seeking a better life for themselves and their families. The Donnellys were just more faces in the crowd of humanity that sought to improve their lot in life. But James Donnelly, his wife Johannah, and their son James Jr. traveled to Canada under a cloud. Sit down, strap in, and hang on - this one's gonna be a bumpy, complicated ride.

The shocking murders of the Donnelly family left a stain on Canadian history that hasn't faded, even in the present day. On the night of February 3, 1880, long-simmering resentments boiled over into violence. When it was over, five people were dead in two houses, one of which was in flames. How did this happen?

The story begins in Ireland in the middle of the nineteenth century -- and, to be honest, about two hundred years before that, but we'll get to that in a bit. James Donnelly, a squat, stumpy stagecoach driver, fell in love with a tall, strongly-built woman named Johanna Magee. Johanna's father was against this relationship, so James and Johannah eloped. Then around 1842, James went off to Canada to seek his fortune. A lot of families from Tipperary were emigrating to Biddulph Township, near Lucan in Ontario. James fetched up in London, Ontario, and started working, trying to build up enough funds to bring his new wife to the New World to join him.

Meanwhile, Johannah discovered that she was pregnant. This gave her a bit of leverage over her father, who was still angry about the whole situation. She gave birth to a son, whom she named James, Jr. She took the baby to her father and said, "Look, this kid's going to grow up without a father unless I go and find my husband. Is that what you want for your grandson?" Her father admitted that no, it wasn't, so he gave her some cash and sent her on her way. Johannah found her way to London,

Ontario, and started looking for James. She found him in a bar, drinking with his buddies after a long day's work.

"Where'd YOU come from?" James sputtered.

"Where'd you GO?!?" was Johannah's retort.

The newlyweds were reunited and started life in London. James continued to work, and in 1844 another son was born. William was born with a deformed foot and would be known all his life by the nickname "Clubfoot Will".

City life held no appeal for James, who wanted to farm the land on which he lived, making a good honest living for his family. The Canada Land Company was offering land in Biddulph Township to Irish settlers, leasing it with an option to buy. But the Donnellys were poor folks, and James knew he could never afford to buy land.

So, he squatted on 100 acres instead. He wasn't alone; it was common practice for poor people to do this, especially on the frontier. James settled on land on the Roman line near Biddulph belonging to an absentee landlord, Patrick Fogarty. Fogarty later sold the land to John Grace, who never registered it. He threw a shanty together and began to clear the land.

James And Johannah Donnelly

Over the years, five more boys would be born to the couple: John, Patrick, Michael, Robert, and Thomas. James made improvements to the shanty, turning it into a cozy cabin. All went well until 1855, when John Grace -- you know, the rightful owner of the property -- sold the southern 50 acres of his land to Michael Maher for £200.

James was furious at the impending loss of "his" land. He'd worked hard clearing that land, and he felt he deserved to be able to stay on it. He dared anyone to take the southern fifty acres from him. Surprisingly, no one challenged him.

No one, that is, except Patrick Farrell.

In 1857, Farrell had rented the land from Michael Maher, the new absentee owner. But when he showed up to claim the land, James told him to go pound sand. They went to court over the dispute. The court ruled a tradeoff:

James was allowed to keep the northern 50 acres of the property. But he had to give up the southern half to Farrell. No one knew it yet, but the court had just made a decision that would change Biddulph's history forever.

On June 25, 1857, William Maloney hosted a logging bee. Bees were very common in pioneer days. Going on the maxim "many hands make light work", they were a way for neighbors to help each other with tasks that needed attention. There were logging bees, quilting bees, corn-shucking bees, and barn-raising bees. These were also opportunities for socializing and, of course, drinking.

James Donnelly and Patrick Farrell were both invited to this logging bee, and they both showed up. The booze had been flowing, and most of the farmers were tipping the bottle. So, it's not really clear how the fight started - but everyone there knew that Donnelly and Farrell detested each other. Words were exchanged, which led to violence. Farrell threw a punch; James jabbed back, then decided Farrell wasn't worth his time. He turned his back and started to walk away. Farrell grabbed up a tool called a handspike, a heavy chunk of metal bigger than a railroad spike, and went after James again. Donnelly grabbed one too, to defend himself. Moments later, Patrick Farrell was lying on the ground, with a handspike jammed into his left temple. He died two days later.

James Donnelly was now a murderer. A warrant was issued for his arrest, but when constables showed up at the Donnelly farm, James was nowhere to be found. He stayed hidden for the next 11 months. No one had any idea where he was -- except for Johannah and their three oldest sons. Officers showed up to the farm on the regular, trying to find James to arrest him. But the Donnellys weren't talking.

As it turned out, James had been hiding in plain sight, on his own homestead all along. Sharp-eyed observers might have noticed another woman working the Donnelly fields; they might have, but they didn't. James had disguised himself in his wife's dresses to be able to work next to her in their fields without attracting too much attention. He spent time hidden in the houses of sympathetic neighbors -- and some time in his own house too: their final child, a girl named Jennie, was born at this time. But winters in Ontario are bitterly cold, and after spending one of them sleeping in stables or sheltered in the homes of sympathetic friends, James decided not to spend another one outdoors. In August 1858, James turned himself in.

James hired one of the best lawyers in the province, but even so, he was found guilty, and sentenced to death by hanging. The execution was set for September 17, 1859.

Johannah was devastated by the news, but she was not about to lose her beloved husband, and see her children left fatherless, without a fight. She started up a petition for a lighter sentence, and she had people sign it everywhere she went. Johannah was very well-respected in the community: she started up a school for neighborhood children on their homestead and was well-known for her love of children. Perhaps having seven of her own helped. In addition to that, after Patrick Farrell's death, Johannah and James took in Farrell's son, adopted him, and raised him as their own. In July 1859, her persistence paid off. In the *London Free Press* account of that day, it is reported that Patrick Farrell had attacked James Donnelly with his fists. James defended himself with his fists and knocked Farrell down, then was walking away when Farrell picked up a logging handspike and attacked James from behind. James then defended himself with another handspike and Farrell was killed. Eventually, the hanging sentence was commuted on appeal, because the killing was self-defense. Instead of being hanged, he was sentenced to seven years in Kingston Penitentiary. He was released in 1865.

He came home to a houseful of wild boys. Without the guiding hand of a father, his sons were, to tell the truth, running loose. Johannah had her hands full trying to keep them in line, raise Jennie, and keep the homestead going. Fortunately, the boys were now old enough to start finding jobs. All the Donnelly boys were handsome, astute

in business, unafraid to get into a fight, and notorious womanizers -- which didn't help their reputation in the community. In addition, all the boys, except for Will, were scrappers.

Bob and Tom Donnelly

James Jr. died at the age of 36; rumors were that he had been shot. And Michael was killed in a bar fight at the age of 29.

In May 1873, William Donnelly started up a stagecoach business. "Clubfoot Will" was generally agreed to be the smartest of the Donnelly brothers. Will drew on his father's stagecoach experience from Ireland, and the Donnelly stagecoach line was soon a roaring success. Brothers Will, Michael, John, and Thomas operated the line, which ran between Lucan, Exeter, and London, Ontario. It soon began to rival the government mail stage, which had started in 1838.

The Donnellys' rival for the stage business was the Hawkshaw line, which soon began to crumble under pressure from the competition. In October 1873, Hawkshaw knuckled under and sold his business to Patrick Flanagan. Flanagan was determined to run his fellow Irishmen out of business.

The Stagecoach Feud, between the Donnelly Stagecoach and the Flanagan & Crawly Stage, erupted in Biddulph, sweeping the area with violence. Coaches were smashed, wrecked, and burned, stables were torched, and horses were savagely beaten and even killed. The Donnellys somehow got the blame for most of this violence, and the family began to get a bad reputation.

Here's one example of many -- in 1875, one of Flanagan's stages was destroyed and stage driver William Brooks was killed when a wheel fell off. It was assumed by all that the accident was a result of sabotage. Robert McLeod, who worked for Flanagan, cut off the Donnelly stage on the road, causing passengers to fall out of the carriage. Will Donnelly charged him and received damages. The passengers, Louisa and Martha Lindsay, turned around and charged the Donnellys for dumping them out of the stage, and the Donnellys were forced to pay damages to them.

The anger generated by the Stagecoach Feud spread, and soon the Donnellys were being accused of everything from trespassing to assaulting a police officer to attempted murder. This all makes them sound like a bunch of jerks, but these types of crime were normal for frontier communities. It's just that the Donnellys got blamed for everything.

According to a contemporary newspaper account, if a housewife left a pie to cool on her porch, and a dog stole it, the Donnellys would get blamed. And it wasn't just the Donnelly men who were accused. Johannah would quite often swear a blue streak at police constables, especially Constable James Carroll.

Unfortunately, feuds like this were a way of life in Biddulph. The Roman line, the main road through the area, which ran right past the Donnelly farmhouse, was named for the Roman Catholics who settled in Biddulph. The Biddulph feud had begun in Ireland some two centuries before James Donnelly was born. Biddulph was settled mainly by Irish immigrants, who brought the long-standing bitterness between Catholics and Protestants with them to the New World.

Things really began to heat up in June 1879. Father John Connolly, pastor of St. Patrick's Catholic Church, created a "Peace Society" in Biddulph. He asked members of his congregation to sign a pledge of support, which included an agreement to let society members search their homes for stolen property. The Donnellys did not sign the pledge. Fr. Connolly didn't like the Donnellys anyway. He came to the community and heard the horror stories before he met the family for himself. He formed a bad opinion of them right from the jump. Will wrote to him to explain that his family wasn't all that bad, and that the priest should give them a fair shake, but Fr. Connolly was unmoved in his prejudice.

James was quite liberal -- he even donated money to help build an Anglican church, which did not endear him to Fr. Connolly or the Peace Society. One Sunday, though, Fr. Connolly really ticked James off. The Catholic priest was in the pulpit preaching hatred against Protestants. The Donnellys had many Protestant friends. James stood up in the middle of Mass, denounced Connolly for his unchristian attitude, and proclaimed that from then on, he and his family would attend the Catholic church in London.

In August 1879, a splinter group of the Peace Society, also organized by Fr. Connolly, started meeting in Biddulph. They called themselves the Vigilance Committee, and they really had it in for the Donnellys. They met regularly at the Cedar Swamp Schoolhouse -- incidentally, the same school for which Johannah had provided the land.

Not long after the Vigilance Committee was formed, a cow went missing from the farm of William and Mary Thompson, a black couple. The Vigilance Committee immediately accused the Donnellys of the theft and searched the farm for the missing cow. James Carroll led the search. The cow was later found at the Thompson's farm, right where she belonged. The Donnellys accused the Vigilance Committee of trespassing. Back and forth, back and forth ...

The spark that touched off the final confrontation came on January 15, 1880. Patrick "Grouchy" Ryder's barn burned down. Everyone -- spurred on by the Peace Society -- blamed the Donnellys. Actually, some of the incidents of arson, property damage and violence in Biddulph at the time was in fact the work of the Peace Society. There was absolutely no evidence that pointed to the Donnellys being the arsonists, and all the Donnelly boys had been at a wedding the night the barn burned. So, James and Johannah were blamed. Ryder himself said that he'd been neighbor to the Donnellys for over 30 years and had never had an issue with them, and that the only reason he sent constables after them was that they were regularly blamed for everything.

Father Connolly stepped up to the pulpit at St. Patrick's and spoke to his congregation. He said that an evil had fallen on the community, and that $500 would be offered as a reward for getting rid of the wicked. Since there was zero legal evidence linking the Donnellys to the burning of Grouchy Ryder's barn, members of the community decided to take the law into their own hands.

On the morning of February 3, James Donnelly sat down at the kitchen table with his son Tom, and with Tom's help, drafted a letter to his lawyer regarding the Ryder arson

A contemporary illustration showing the Donnelly home at the time of the first attack by the Vigilance Committee.

case. The Donnellys were expected in court the next day. James wrote to the lawyer outlining the facts of the case: Grouchy had been their neighbor for 30 years and they'd never had any trouble, and there was no evidence to suggest that he and Johannah had set the fire. He added, "It seems hard to see a man and woman over 60 years of age dragged around as laughingstock."

The day went on as usual, with James, Jr., John, and Tom leaving around 4:00 p.m. to pick up a neighbor boy, Johnny O'Connor. Johnny often helped the Donnellys with farm chores, and it was not unusual for him to come and stay with the family. This time, Johnny was to care for the pigs while the family was in Granton for the court appearance.

When they got back to the house, John and Tom put the horse away, then John left to visit Will, who lived at Whalen's Corners. Johnny fed the pigs and did more chores in the barn. Around 10:00 p.m., a neighbor, Jim Feeheley, stopped in to say hello, but didn't stay long. Then everyone settled down for the night.

The Donnelly house was small, so Johnny bunked with James in the front bedroom. Johanna slept in her own room, sharing her bed with Bridget, her niece, who was visiting from Ireland. Tom had his own bed in a little room off the kitchen.

Around midnight on February 3, members of the Vigilance Committee gathered at the Cedar Swamp Schoolhouse to get liquored up before heading out to the Donnelly homestead. The group included Grouchy Ryder, whose barn had been torched, and James Carroll, one of the constables Johannah Donnelly was known to swear at. In all, 35 men showed up at the Donnelly home that night, thirsting for blood. Jim Feeheley's earlier visit had really been a scouting trip, to see where each Donnelly was in the house. He didn't notice Johnny O'Connor, so the boy's presence went unreported.

James Carroll came quietly into the house, took handcuffs out of his pocket, and handcuffed Tom Donnelly while Tom was still asleep. Then he woke Tom up and told him he was under arrest. Things escalated very quickly from that point. Carroll frog-marched Tom into the kitchen. Johannah and Bridget woke up and came into the kitchen too. James Sr. soon joined them, asking Carroll "What have you got against us now?" Carroll responded that more charges were being filed against them. James noticed the handcuffs on Tom, and asked, "You are handcuffed?"

"Yes," Tom replied, nodding at Carroll, "he thinks he's smart." Then, as if taunting Carroll further, Tom demanded, "Read the warrant."

They were the last words he would ever speak.

At a signal from Carroll, the men outside stormed the house. They were all armed with sticks, clubs, and various farm tools, and they began beating the three adults. Bridget broke free and ran upstairs. Johnny, unnoticed by the attackers, followed her up the stairs, but Bridget didn't notice him either, and inadvertently slammed the door in his face. Johnny fled back down the stairs and hid under the bed in the front bedroom, where he'd been sleeping.

James Donnelly was the first to fall; the men beat him in the head, pulping his skull. Johannah was also bludgeoned to death. Tom, 25-years-old and strong, fought hard to protect himself and his family. He made it just outside the front door, where Tom Ryder was waiting for him with a pitchfork. He savaged Tom Donnelly, stabbing him in the chest with the sharp tines over and over. Once Tom was down, the men carried him back into the kitchen where his parents' bodies lay, and took the handcuffs off

him. Tom was still alive, and groaning. Someone said, "Hit that fellow on the head and break his skull open." One of the men, either Jim Toohey or Patrick Quigley, bashed Tom's head with a shovel three or four times.

The men realized that Bridget Donnelly was missing. They found her upstairs and killed the 21-year-old girl, too. The Donnellys' dog wouldn't stop barking at all the commotion, so one of the men smashed the dog's head with a shovel, killing it.

Then they went to the front bedroom, poured coal oil all over the bed under which Johnny lay quivering with terror, and lit the bed on fire, hoping that the whole house would soon catch.

Then the men went hunting for more Donnellys.

Will Donnelly lived with his wife Nora in Whalen's Corners, not far from the Donnelly homestead. On that night, he and Nora had two visitors, Will's brother John, and Martin Hogan, a friend. John was there to borrow a sleigh for the ride into Granton for court the next day, and Martin had just come for a visit. Martin and John were both invited to stay the night. Nora went to bed around 9:00 p.m., and the men stayed up talking, finally turning in around 12:30 a.m.

Nora was about six months pregnant at the time, and not feeling her best. When Will came in to bed, he asked Nora to roll over next to the wall, so he could get into bed. She sleepily protested, saying she didn't want to

A postcard that was sold depicting some of the victims of the Vigilance Massacre of the "Black" Donnellys.

leave her warm spot. So, Will climbed over her. That small concession to Nora's comfort probably saved Will's life.

Will had been asleep for about two hours when he was awakened by John coming through his bedroom on the way to the kitchen and back door. Will groggily registered that someone outside was yelling his name and shouting about fire. "Fire! Fire! Open the door, Will!"

The calls from outside weren't a warming, they were a ploy to get Will to come outside to be shot. The mob had thrown away all pretense of stealth at that point. They were out for Will's blood; he was considered the smartest of the Donnelly brothers, and the mob wanted him dead. They surrounded the house, but instead of storming inside, they tried to get Will to come out. They broke into the barn and led Will's prize stallion out, and started beating it savagely, hoping that the horse's screams would draw Will out of the house.

But it was John who opened the door -- and was cut down by several blasts from a shotgun. John dropped with 30 holes in his chest and groin. The shots pierced his lung and broke his collarbone and several ribs. Nora tried to move John to safety, but he was too heavy for her to drag. Martin helped her drag John to the bedroom, where Nora forced his hand closed around a piece of blessed candle. John, just 32-years-old, died within five minutes of being shot.

After milling around for a while longer, the mob drifted away. Will, Nora, and Martin huddled on the floor next to John's cooling body until the dawn broke.

Meanwhile, a short distance away, the Donnelly home continued to burn. Johnny had wriggled out from under the bed as soon as the mob left and ran to Patrick Whalen's cabin next door. Whalen took the boy in but warned him not to speak of the killings. The Donnelly cabin was soon engulfed in flames. The second floor collapsed, sending Bridget's body tumbling into the kitchen to join the others. Falling snow eventually covered the crime scene, snuffing out the flames. Investigators later piled the charred remains of all four Donnellys into one coffin for the funeral service.

Will and Nora Donnelly and Martin Hogan all recognized the men who had killed John Donnelly. One of them was John Kennedy, Nora's brother. And young Johnny O'Connor witnessed the whole horrible scene at the Donnelly farmhouse. Will and Patrick Donnelly spent all their time leading up to the trial searching the community for more witnesses. But no one was ever punished for the two-part massacre, despite Johnny's court testimony. The authorities in Biddulph simply covered the whole thing up.

Eventually, six men were tried for the Donnelly murders: James Carroll, the constable who ran afoul of Johannah; John Purtell; Thomas Ryder, Grouchy's brother; James Ryder, Jr.; Martin McLaughlin; and John Kennedy, Will Donnelly's brother-in-law. All the men backed up each other's alibis. One juror said that he wouldn't have convicted even if he'd seen the murders done himself. Another didn't

James Carroll, the constable who often ran afoul of Johannah Donnelly.

want to convict just on the testimony of a 12-year-old boy. The rest were afraid of the defendants. The press were pretty firmly on Will and Patrick's side, and described Carroll and the others as "a bunch of envious, dangerous backwoodsmen." The first trial ended with a hung jury: seven to acquit, four to convict, and one undecided.

In the second trial, James Carroll was tried first -- the prosecutor figured that if he was convicted, there was a better chance of getting more convictions down the line. Carroll had been the first one into the Donnelly cabin, and he stood accused of the murders of James and Johannah. Johnny O'Connor was called to the stand to testify, but his eyewitness testimony was largely ignored. His mother was also called. But the defense argued that Johnny's mother had asked the court for money, and therefore her testimony was suspect, as was her son's. They conveniently ignored the fact that Johnny's mother had, indeed, asked for money -- because their house had been burned down in retribution for their court appearance. They really did need the help. James Carroll walked away from the trial a free man. Without his conviction, there was no reason to try the other five men, and they were released on bail.

The surviving Donnellys were incredibly magnanimous towards some of the people involved in their family's murder. Will and Patrick befriended Jim Feeheley, who scouted out the cabin that fateful night. He confessed to Patrick the part he'd played in the evening's gruesome events. He said he was afraid of the Vigilance Committee. In April 1881, Jim and Michael Feeheley fled to Michigan, but were extradited back to Canada in September and charged with aiding and abetting the murder of Tom Donnelly. They refused to testify against anyone, so the prospect of a third trial fizzled out. The Crown agreed to let them go on bail, which was paid for by -- wait for it -- the Vigilance Committee.

The Donnelly property still bears the psychic imprint of the ghastly crime. The paranormal activity on the land is extreme. Horses seem to be especially sensitive to the psychic residue. Horses ridden near the property late at night on February 3 will refuse to go any further or go berserk as if possessed. If they are forced to go any further after balking, the horses soon die mysteriously. This has happened to at least three mounts.

The weirdness doesn't stop with the doomed horses. Blue balls of lightning have been seen rolling down the road next to the Donnelly land on the anniversary of the killings.

Photographs of the Donnelly tombstones on the property show strange figures and light anomalies.

Robert and Linda Salts moved into the Donnelly house in 1988 and began experiencing paranormal activity on the very first day. The original house no longer stands, of course. In 1881, a year after the massacre, some of the surviving family members, sons Will, James Jr., Patrick, and Robert, restored the middle part of the house. The rest of the house was built around this.

The Salts family hear footsteps going up the stairs late at night, and shadowy figures move through the house constantly. The ghosts of James and Johannah are dressed austerely in somber black, while the spirits of the Donnelly sons appear in white clothes. Will's ghost can sometimes be seen in the yard behind the house, as that was a favorite place of his.

Even the barn, built in 1877, is haunted. Tourists visiting the barn have experienced a heavy feeling pressing down on their chests. Visitors have also reported phantom footsteps, and, more chillingly, the sound of screams.

People in Ontario still speak in whispers of the Donnelly murders. It's been more than 140 years, but the crime was so heinous that it still reverberates today. Add to that the fact that the murderers, although well-known to all, were never brought to justice, and you have a story that deserves to live on in infamy.

MY HAUNTED HOMETOWN

Neighborhood Tales from Groton, New York

A NEW FEATURE FROM THE MORBID CURIOUS THAT HIGHLIGHTS THE HAUNTED HOMETOWNS OF OUR READERS. WANT TO SEND IN YOURS?

ADAM SEAMAN

Groton, New York, isn't a town anyone has ever really heard of, unless you're talking about the one in Connecticut. The town was incorporated in 1860 and at one point was "Typewriter Capital of the World" but like many Upstate New York towns these days, Groton is a shell of its former self. The heart and life force of the town, Smith-Corona Typewriter Company, left as did the railroad and what was once a bustling little industrial powerhouse in the middle of cow country became a hollowed-out ghost to be forgotten and left behind. And for the most part that is the case except for what I know I've experienced growing up there. The living has forgotten the town, but the dead are trying really hard not to.

When I was about 7-years-old roughly, my family and I moved into an unassuming two-family Italianate house on route 222 more or less in the center of town. We lived on the 1st floor. Years later after we had moved out, this place would haunt my dreams.

Yup, I grew up in a haunted house.

The village of Groton, New York and the road I grew up on, living in a haunted house.

Phantom footsteps, bumps in the night, loud raps that seem to come from nowhere and everywhere all at once, Balls bouncing on the ceiling, cold spots, etc. You name it and it was happening there.   Most menacing, besides the general feeling of the house, was one night when my mother flew off the couch and frantically dialed 911 because she saw the cellar door bulging out from its hinges as if someone were trying like hell to get into the house. When the police arrived, they found no one, no tracks in the snow, no nothing. Sometime later, after we have moved out, I started piecing together things about the place that seemed odd -- the covered stairway to the second floor in the back of the house that went from the driveway to the upstairs kitchen, the parlor doors that led to the master bedroom, the mourning bench out in the side lawn

and then it hit me: We lived in what used to be a funeral home! Or at least that is what I thought. Rumor has it a man hanged himself in the garage on the property there in the 1960s. Perhaps the activity was linked to that sad chapter in the house's history.

I was a strange kid, or so society thought. I liked my music heavy, and it was the 90's. My favorite place to hang out, with the living or the dead was, of course, the local cemetery. The kids at school even nicknamed me "Graveyard" I was seen there so often. The original cemetery in town was down on the south end of Main St. But was moved up on the top of Clark Street in 1858. There is only one mausoleum up there, that of Dr. Miles D. Goodyear and his wife, Emma. The family must have held some prominence in town. The mausoleum has a broken stained-glass window in the back and me and my friends would set up a voice recorder there and ask questions, hoping to get a response. Besides various unexplained knocks and bangs, we actually recorded a few sounds that we thought were people talking.

"Come and lay down with her," an old man seemed to say as if straight out of a Dicken's Christmas Carol. Another, in a female voice said, "Jessica... What's that?" It wouldn't be weird except that we were always standing right there, as silent as those around us, or so we thought.

That isn't the end of my experiences here, though. One day, me and my good friend Nick were walking up to the cemetery. We had gone downtown for a snack and were planning to hang out up in the boneyard. I had my "boom box" that day and was playing Godsmack. As we were entering the grounds, I looked up and saw a man at a stone. He was wearing what looked like dark grey khakis or dress pants that one might have worn everyday back when that was a thing and a white undershirt. Now I may have been a metalhead, but I wasn't disrespectful, I turned down the boom box. As we continued to walk in, he started for the same driveway to walk out and he was going to pass us. "Well, this is awkward," I thought.

I followed him out of the corner of my eye and as he went to pass us, I looked up to nod at him and acknowledge his presence.

He was gone.

It was as though he'd never been there at all. My buddy Nick, who was in front of me, never saw him.

Another time, another buddy and I were walking up to the cemetery from the cornfield and stumbled on a woman, dressed in black, kneeling at a grave somewhere in the newer section of the cemetery. She had candles and other things with her all over the grave. When she saw us, she quickly packed up her stuff and scurried away down the road away from town. We didn't stick around to see where she went.

There is a trail that runs through the middle of town. It used to be the local branch of the Southern Central and then Lehigh Valley Railroads. The station in town still stands near where the Ice Cream Caboose is. The tracks are no longer there and a train hasn't passed through to pick up passengers in decades.

One late night, I was talking online to my best friend from across the street and I asked him if he wanted to go for a midnight stroll, something we often did. He was game and said to meet him outside. Before I could even get out of my chair, he was frantically texting me to get outside quickly but when I asked him why, he wouldn't tell me. He liked to leave you hanging. Annoyed with him, I took my time getting out there.

"Did you hear it?", he asked.

"Hear what?" I replied.

"The ghost train," he answered.

I'd never heard of any ghost train around town. I considered myself a history buff and, by this time, was well acquainted with the hauntings and lore of the town. I had never heard anyone speak of or mention anything about a ghost train. Surely that would be something everyone knew about. We started for our walk. No more than five minutes passed before we both stopped

What's left of the Lehigh Valley Railroad tracks that run through the middle of town. It's along these "tracks" that the ghost train still runs.

road. There was nothing in the sky above. It just seemed to emanate from the blackness.

We listened to it for several minutes and then suddenly I got the idea to rush down to Walpole Road. This was where the tracks crossed. I wanted to see if we could see anything that would explain the noise. Before we made it down to the main road going out of town, though, the sound had stopped. Undeterred, we continued towards where the old tracks used to be. Once we made it to Walpole Road, it was well past midnight. A house, one of the few on the road before the tracks, had lights on and two men were outside.

"Let's go ask these guys if they heard it, too" I said to my buddy. We went over and I asked the guy closest to us. "This is kind of a weird question -- but by any chance did you just hear a train?"

He rubbed his chin and giggled. "See, I told you I wasn't crazy," he said to his buddy who was coming out of his garage.

"Maybe it was the ghost train," his friend shrugged, reinforcing the idea that I must have been the only person around town who wasn't familiar with that story. Although at least I am now!

dead in our tracks. Out in the darkness of the town, we heard what sounded clearly like the horn of a train. We were up on a hill, literally just outside the village line. Groton sits between two hills, so on either side of you it's just woods everywhere. The sound continued. We just stopped and listened. The horn didn't move so it wasn't a car or semi-truck down on the

Near where the "Ghost Train" incident occurred, my same friend and myself went on one of our signature "blizzard walks" one night. Like many true male humans, we liked to go out for early evening walks in driving snowstorms - which are pretty common in rural New York in the winter.

On this particular night, it was under truly blizzard conditions. Visibility was maybe 50-100 yards. While walking from the same stretch of road from my driveway to Walpole Road - secretly still hoping to catch a glimpse of the spectral steam engine that had been the highlight of another late-night walk - we trudged along through the storm.

"Hey, what's that?" my buddy nudged me.

I looked up to see this ball of light maybe 100 yards in front of us just dancing around the road right at Chipman's Corners. It moved, danced around, and turned in circles.

We watched it for a few seconds, and it disappeared. We hurried up to the spot where we thought we'd seen it, looking for any explanation but there was none to be had. The roads were covered in snow but there were no footprints nearby. The wind was howling, the snow was coming down, and there didn't appear to be anyone other than we two geniuses out in the storm. I looked up and down the road but saw no one. It was certainly a weird experience. What has caused it?

What came to my mind almost immediately was a tragic accident that occurred not more than a couple of years prior in the same spot.

A woman - the daughter of one of my neighbors -- was struck and killed by a semi-truck as she rushed to the hospital to see the birth of her nephew. She died on the spot. Her nephew was born shortly after.

Could this have been a "spook light" of some sort? Her presence left behind there? Her accident wasn't the first at Chipman's Corners and won't be the last.

The accident takes us back to the town cemetery. My neighbor showed me a picture of her family spending time at the gravesite of her daughter - with an extra person in the frame. A smudge that appeared over the shoulder of a family member contained a perfect likeness of the dead daughter's face! There was no way to deny that she seemed to be there with them.

Other places in town said to be haunted include the local library, an old church, and "The Mansion on the Hill". I've never personally experienced anything at those locations, but I've heard stories. With all that I've seen in town, I have no reason to doubt them.

Groton was a great place to grow up in and my spooky experiences made it that much more memorable. Maybe that's why we have so many restless spirits in Groton. Maybe they think it's a great place, too.

THE GHOST IN THE BELFRY

Hauntings of Virginia's Aquia Church

REGARDED AS ONE OF THE MOST FAMOUS
HAUNTED PLACES IN THE STATE, THIS EPSICOAL
CHURCH HAS SEEN MORE THAN ITS SHARE OF HISTORY!

MICHELLE L. HAMILTON

Aquia Episcopal Church

The beautiful and historic Aquia Episcopal Church has been the heart of the community since 1667. Located in Stafford County, Virginia in Overwharton Parish, Aquia Church is oldest established church in the county. Today, visitors and congregants continue to gather to worship at Aquia Church in the historic structure that dates to the 1750s. Aquia Church has a fascinating history and has witnessed the birth of the nation and the destruction of the Civil War. Naturally, such an historic structure has also acquired a few ghostly tales.

In 1667, Aquia Church was established to serve the spiritual needs of Overwharton Parish. During the colonial period, the Anglican Church was the official religion of the Virginia colony. Colonists were required to attend services at their local parish church and were taxed by the parish to maintain and support the church. Aquia Church took its name from the nearby Aquia Creek and was placed off the main road - now Telegraph Road - of Stafford County that allowed for easy access to the site.

The original structure was a simple wooden chapel, but by the mid-1700s the parish decided a new, finer, structure was needed. Construction of the church began in 1751 and continued until 1755 when disaster struck. As reported in *The Virginia Gazette* on March 21, 1755:

"We hear from Stafford County, that the new Church at Aquia, one of the best Building in the Colony (and the old wooden one near it) were burnt down on the 17th Instant, by the carelessness of some of the Carpenters leaving Fire too near the Shavings, at Night, when they left off Work. This fine Building was within two or three Days Work of being compleatly (sic.) finished and delivered up by the Undertakers..."

The structure was quickly rebuilt and in 1757 the structure was completed. Built with Flemish bond brickwork with Aquia sandstone that was acquired from the local quarry from Government Island, the structure is an elegant building.

Aquia Church withstood the turmoil of the American Revolution and the establishment of the Episcopal Church in the United States. After the war, church membership declined following the Virginia Statute for Religious Freedom that was enacted in 1786. The statute granted Virginians the freedom to worship where they saw fit. As a result, attendance at Aquia Church shrank. For the first half of the 19th-century, the church struggled to attract new members. By the 1850s, things began to look brighter as a new rector brought life back to the

A rare example of a Memento Mori style marker in the cemetery at Aquia Episcopal Church.

old church. The rebirth of Aquia Church was threatened by the Civil War. Aquia Church was occupied by both Confederate and Union soldiers between 1861-1865. The structure was protected during the Union occupation of Stafford County by Army chaplain Reverend Henry Wheeler who used Aquia Church to hold religious services for Union soldiers.

Despite the best efforts of Rev. Wheeler, the war still left its toll on Aquia Church. Solider graffiti from both sides were etched on the church walls, windows were missing, pews had been chewed by cavalry horses, and gravestones in the church cemetery had been disinterred to build fireplaces. Like a phoenix rising from the ashes, Aquia Church was restored to its former glory and continues to serve the spiritual needs of Stafford County.

With such a rich and colorful history, it is to be expected that the site

The marks left behind by Civil War soldiers. The soldiers carved their names in the soft Aquia sandstone. The above inscription reads: "CMcC. 5 Tex Vol 1862."

has a few ghostly legends attached to it. In the 1930s, paranormal researcher Marguerite Dupont Lee visited Aquia Church and interviewed parishioners about the church. The tale they related has the hallmark of a gothic novel. According to the legend, following the Revolutionary War a beautiful young woman was murdered in the church by highwaymen. To cover up their bloody dead, the highwaymen hid her body inside the church's belfry. Since then, the story goes, the restless spirit of the murdered woman wanders the church at midnight.

The story became ingrained in the community to such an extent that according to Lee, "that under no circumstances could any man in Stafford County be induced to enter the church at night." It should be noted that there is no evidence in the historic record to corroborate the legend of the murdered woman. Regardless of the lack of documentation, many in Stafford County believed that there was a ghost at Aquia Church.

"Everyone speaks of sounds in the church as though someone was running up and down stairs. A number of people have heard heavy noises, suggesting a struggle was taking place. Upon entering – all is quiet," Agnes Moncure recounted to Lee.

In her research, Lee uncovered a story that suggested that the ghost of Aquia Church was a helpful spirit. During the Civil War, two young Confederate soldiers, William Fitzhugh and an unnamed companion decided to spend the night at Aquia Church after spending the day scouting the terrain. The young men decided to make their beds in the church pews, but their rest was disturbed by the sounds of footsteps at the rear of the church on the stone flagging. Then Fitzhugh and his friend heard the tune "The Campbells are Coming" being whistled. The whistling and footsteps drew closer to the soldiers. Upon the approach of the footsteps, the soldiers struck a light to reveal that they were alone.	Unnerved by the sounds, Fitzhugh decided to check the church door when they spotted Union soldiers approaching.	The Confederates had just enough time to jump out of a window.	According to Lee, for the remainder of his life Fitzhugh "always attributed their escape to the whistling of the ghost."

Aquia Church is open to the public as a historic landmark and as an active church. Visitors are welcome to attend worship services or to arrange a tour of the church.

Works Cited
"About," Aquia Church
"Decline & Revival of Independence"
"Early Parish History"
"The Civil War at Aquia Church"
https://aquiachurch.org/about/history/

Marguerite Dupont Lee, *Virginia Ghosts,* Berryville, VA, Virginia Book Company, 1966

The Virginia Gazette, Hunter: March 21, 1755,
https://research.history.org/DigitalLibrary/va-gazettes/VGSinglePage.cfm?IssueIDNo=55.H.05&page=3.

The Man Who Was Buried Standing Up

One of the weirdest legends of Southwest Virginia is told about an old tomb that is located just past the town of Elliston. The man interred in the tomb was Colonel George Hancock, a dashing and slightly eccentric gentleman who served as a Virginia congressman during George Washington's administration. He fought during the Revolutionary War and after, retired in Elliston to run his plantation. He was a man of bad temperament who never trusted his slaves and when he died, he asked to be entombed standing up. The reason for this, he stated, was so that he could watch over his slaves "and keep them from loafing on the job."

Over the years, the tomb was disturbed many times. Curiosity seekers explored it, searching for evidence of the legend's truth and soldiers even broke into it during the Civil War to see the body of Colonel Hancock. Today, trees, dense underbrush and wild rose bushes hide the crypt, which has fallen into scattered ruins. But even so, the story remains.

Was there any truth to it? Many believe there was, including a man who was a gardener what had been Hancock's plantation in the early and middle 1900's. He had lived in the area all his life and as a child used to play near the old tomb. One look inside had convinced the young boy that Colonel Hancock had indeed been entombed in a way that allowed him to look out over his estate.

The other great believers in the tale were the Hancock slaves, who toiled on the plantation until the end of the Civil War. It was said that they worked even harder after his death than before. Many of them scoffed at the idea that Hancock could watch over them after death, but they weren't taking any chances!

THE LAST AMERICAN VAMPIRE

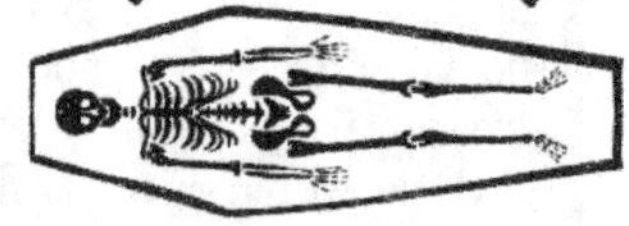

The True Story of Mercy Brown

TROY TAYLOR

On the cold morning of March 17, 1892, a group of men marched down Purgatory Road in the town of Exeter, Rhode Island. They were walking to Chestnut Hill Cemetery. Their intention was not to witness the burial of a loved one, but rather to remove the coffins of the dead from the ground. But were those they sought truly dead? Or had they returned in some way to prey on the living? This is what they hoped to learn from their journey to the graveyard. In this case, the life of a young man named Edwin Brown - and perhaps the lives of the rest of his remaining family - might depend on it.

Edwin Brown, many believed, had become the prey of a vampire. His life had literally been drained away from him. In such danger that he fled to Colorado to escape; he had returned to Rhode Island when his health did not improve. He was now resigned to the fact that he would die among family and friends, but there were those who believed he could be saved. If they could find the vampire that was stealing his life, he might recover.

It all depended on a macabre ritual - a "certain cure" for vampire victims that had been written about in 1784 by a Willington County, Connecticut, resident named Moses Holmes. The "cure" required that the body of a dead relative be disinterred and that any part of the deceased that is not decomposed be burned, and then consumed by the victim. In those days, it was believed that vampires did not prowl the night looking for victims among strangers -- they drained the life from surviving family members instead. By searching the graves of Brown family members who had already died, Edwin's friends and family members believed that they might find the culprit that was sending the young man into his own early grave.

Edwin's father, George Brown, had buried his wife and his two daughters over the course of nearly 10 years and now it looked as though his son was lost to him, as well. Nevertheless, George put no stock in the ghoulish superstition that some claimed might save Edwin's life. As time passed, though, he was at last convinced to allow the ritual to proceed. He loved his son and planned to accompany him to the cemetery that morning, but at the last moment, balked at the idea of exhuming the graves of the three women. If one of them truly was a vampire, he was unable to face it.

The group of would-be vampire hunters adjourned to the local cemetery, carrying with them a collection of picks and shovels for the grim work ahead. The body of Edwin's sister, Mercy, would be much easier to obtain. She had died only two months earlier, on January 12, and her body had been placed inside of a stone receiving crypt on the cemetery grounds so that she could be buried when the ground began to thaw for the season.

The exhumation that occurred that day might have never come to public attention if the family did not seek out official sanction for their plan. They approached the district medical examiner, Dr. Harold Metcalf, to oversee the uncovering of the corpses. Metcalf, who "acted under protest, as it were being an unbeliever," stated a letter about the incident that appeared in a local newspaper, was an intelligent young man who didn't believe Edwin's illness had anything to do with a vampire. He did all that he could to discourage the exhumation but since it was not technically against the law, there was little he could do. He watched in horror as the men opened the graves of Mary Brown and her eldest daughter, Mary Olive.

The two women had died nearly 10 years before. Mrs. Brown, aged only 36, had died in December 1883 and her 19-year-old daughter had perished just six months later. The men worked long and hard to break through the cold and unforgiving late winter earth. Each of the caskets, now deteriorated with age, were pulled from the ground, and broken open. Both corpses were found, after the passages of years, to be in states of advanced decomposition. There was no question that they had rested in peace during the past nine years. Neither of the two women could be the vampire that was draining the life from young Edwin.

There was no other choice. The coffin of Mercy Brown would also have to be opened.

The stone receiving crypt was located at the edge of the cemetery. It was a triangular-shaped building with a heavy wooden door that was usually kept locked. On this morning, one of the men had obtained the keys from the sexton and the door was opened to reveal a dark, damp interior. The cool smell of earth rushed out at them as they stood in the doorway, allowing their eyes to adjust to the darkness within. Mercy's casket was carried from the crypt and out into the sickly sunlight of the overcast morning. A hasp was broken, and the lid was raised.

In the case of Mrs. Brown and Mary Olive, the doctor and the vampire hunters saw bodies that were "just what might be expected from a similar examination of almost any person after the same length of time" in the grave. But with Mercy, it was a different story. As the men looked down on her body, they saw a face and form that was still very intact. This was not all that strange in that she had only been buried two months before and it had been a cold winter, which would have preserved the body. What was strange, though, was that the corpse had turned onto her side. Obviously, they believed, she had moved -- something that no ordinary corpse could do!

Again, despite protestations from Dr. Metcalf, one of the men cut open the body and found that her heart was still wet with blood. Dr. Metcalf insisted that this as not unusual and was, in fact, consistent with the amount of time that she had been dead, but the men weren't listening. They believed that they finally had all the evidence they needed to show that one of the Browns was indeed a vampire. It was Mercy, they were convinced, and only the prescribed ritual could save the life of her beleaguered brother.

Throwing up his hands in frustration, Dr. Metcalf left the cemetery and left the men to their gruesome work. Atop the nearby stone wall around the cemetery, the men made a fire and burned the heart of Mercy Brown. The fire sputtered and sizzled as it curled around the wet organ, finally reaching temperatures high enough to cause the flesh to scorch and burn. After it had been consumed by the flames, one of the men gathered the ashes and concocted the notorious mixture that was supposed to save Edwin's life.

Edwin -- no doubt with great reluctance -- drank down the horrible mixture.

As it turned out, though, the day's dark work had been carried out in vain. On May 2, he, like his mother and two sisters, died despite all of the efforts to save him.

But perhaps it was not all for nothing. After Edwin's death -- and perhaps because of the destruction of

Mercy's heart -- the vampire never troubled the Brown family again.

The horror was finally over, and Mercy Brown had earned a place in history as the last American vampire.

There is no supernatural creature that fascinates us as much as the vampire does. Although long considered to be nothing more than a myth, the vampire is a still a strangely attractive and enticing being to the modern reader. We think of them as nothing more than the fanciful creation of folklore and literature, but this is not what our ancestors believed. They were convinced that vampires were very real creatures, destroying the lives of the living in ways that are never dreamed of in the fanciful stories that we hear today. They were terrified of these creatures and as you will soon see, it was for very good reason.

Few can really say what the traditional vampire is. Some believe that he is an evil spirit that wears the body of the newly dead, while others believe that he is a corpse, re-animated by his original soul. What everyone can agree on is what this creature must have to survive -- blood. This vital bodily ingredient must be taken from the veins of a living person so that the vampire can survive.

In nearly every case, a vampire that is exhumed from his grave, or resting place, is always found to be ruddy of complexion, well-nourished and apparently in good health. This is even though he had been dead for some time. His appearance is often marked by long, curving fingernails - having grown long in the grave - and blood smeared about the mouth. According to European legends, the only way to destroy one of these living corpses is to drive a stake through its heart. After that, the body should be burned.

The legends of vampires have their roots in traditional fears. In days past, it was not uncommon for people to be fearful about the dead returning from their grave, especially in cases of suicides or of unfortunates being buried without the last rites. Occasional deviants who practiced necrophilia or corpse-stealing often provided apparent "proof" that some of the dead could leave the graveyard. An empty coffin was not seen as evidence of theft, but evidence of vampirism instead.

Terrible and what seemed to be mysterious outbreaks of disease and plagues were sometimes thought to be caused by supernatural means. Probably the most common source of vampire legends, though, came from premature burials. People suffering from catalepsy and other ailments sometimes found themselves buried alive and when later exhumed, the distorted state of the corpses led many

to believe the dead had been coming and going from their coffins for some time. In the eighteenth century, it was not uncommon for bodies to be dug up to see if they had become vampires, especially when it involved the death of a suicide, a murder victim, or someone who had died during a spate of unexplained deaths. If a body was discovered to be in any way out of the ordinary, it was burned to prevent it leaving the grave again.

Vampire-like creatures have existed in the folklore of the world since almost the beginning of recorded history, but a true, traditional vampire was originally a Slavonic monster, bringing fear to the superstitious in Eastern Europe -- Hungary, Czechoslovakia, Rumania, the Balkan countries, and their neighbors. Even the word "vampire" is an adaptation of the Magyar word *vampir*, which also had close ties to Bulgarian and Russian words that mean the same thing. It is believed that the vampire legend began to grow in notoriety around the sixteenth century. Within the next few decades, a considerable spate of vampire activity began to be reported, creating eerie tales and haunting rumors throughout the region.

Soon after, the legend began to spread. A Greek writer, Leone Allacci, produced a small book about vampire belief and other travelers began to pick up stories as they passed through Eastern Europe. Learned clergymen alluded to stories of vampires that were reported to them by parishioners, but in 1746, a Benedictine monk named Don Augustin Calmet published a full-length treatise on ghosts and vampires that firmly planted the legend within the lore of the western world.

The arrival of the vampire in Western Europe was achieved in part by the dissemination of Balkan folk tales, but the process was completed by another important thread in the construction of the legend -- pure fiction. The German romantics of the late eighteenth century found useful images in the horrors of folklore and the use of the vampire motif in poems by Goethe spread the tales ever further. A vampire appeared in a poem by Lord Byron, and in another by Southey, early in the nineteenth century's

English romantic tradition. Oddly, though, none of the earlier writers of "Gothic" horror fiction, like Horace Walpole, Ann Radcliffe, or Matthew Lewis, included vampires int heir eerie tales.

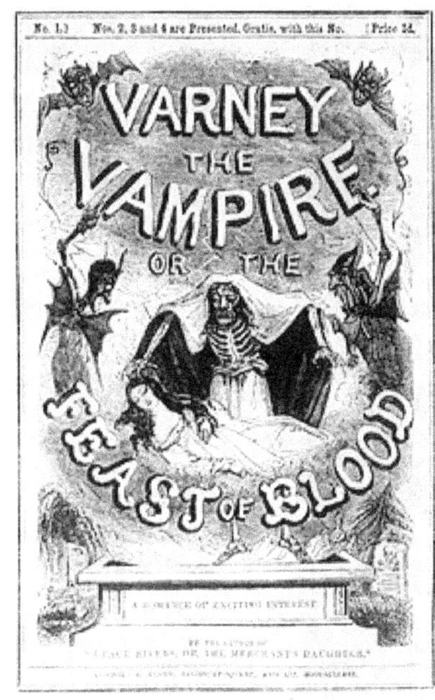

What has been regarded as the first true vampire story was written in 1819 by Dr. John Polidori and it was titled simply "The Vampyre." This short tale was written during the same fateful summer that the 20-year-old Polidori spent with his friend and patient, Lord Byron, along with Percy Shelley and Mary Shelley on the shores of Lake Geneva. A writing contest that summer spawned not only the first vampire story, but Mary Shelley's *Frankenstein*, as well. The short piece appeared in the *New Monthly Magazine*, a British literary journal, and delighted readers with its gloomy atmosphere and its depraved aristocratic vampire, Lord Ruthven, which had been modeled on Lord Byron. It was not one of the finest stories ever written, but it had the advantage of being the first about vampires and, thanks to this, Polidori has earned a place of honor in the annals of horror.

Decades passed and the public gained a taste for blood - at least in a literary sense. In Paris, a play about vampires was one of the most popular theater attractions of the 1820s. Alexandre Dumas wrote a play about vampires in the 1850s, joining other productions that were all the rage across Europe. The French poet, Gautier, used the vampire theme in one of his poems, as did Baudelaire. Then, in 1847, one of the first major written works appeared on the subject in the form of a "penny dreadful" novel by Thomas Preskett Prest called *Varney, the Vampire*. Although it was more than 800 pages long -- it appeared in a series of cheap, penny booklets -- this simple, fast-moving horror story became a sensation with the masses. Vampires, clearly, had come to stay.

One of the most exciting -- and definitely most sensual --- literary vampires of the nineteenth century appeared in a small 1872 novella by Joseph Sheridan Le Fanu called *Carmilla*. It tells the story of a female vampire who gradually seduces a beautiful young girl, causing her health to fail until the sympathetic villain can be dispatched.

Audiences thrilled to Carmilla in the 1870s and the story is considered a classic today. The title character

Bram Stoker, creator of the most famous
literary vampire of all time, Dracula

became the prototype for a legion of female and lesbian vampires. Though Le Fanu portrays his vampire's sexuality with the cautiousness that one would expect for his time, it is evident that sexual attraction is the main dynamic between Carmilla and Laura, the narrator of the story. Carmilla selected exclusively female victims, though only became emotionally involved with a few of them. She was a little different than the accepted form of a vampire in that she had nocturnal habits but was not confined to the darkness. She had unearthly beauty and slept in a coffin, as many of the vampires that followed her would also do.

But there would be no other book that would so affect the literary vampire like the one that came along at the end of the nineteenth century, written by an Irish author named Bram Stoker -- *Dracula*. Stoker's Dracula became a virtual synonym for the vampire; if the ordinary person knows anything about the vampire legend, he probably learned it from the bits and pieces of authentic lore that Stoker included in the book. Stoker studied Balkan folklore while working on his book and included a number of references to regional history. His title character took the name of a historical figure, Transylvanian-born Vlad III Dracula of Wallachia. During the main years of his reign, between 1456 and 1462, "Vlad the Impaler" was said to have killed from 20,000 to 40,000 European civilians -- political rivals, criminals, and anyone else he considered "useless to humanity." His favorite method of death was impaling his victims on a sharp pole.

Stoker came across the name "Dracula" in his reading on Romanian history and decided to use it as the name for his villain. He did some research into the history of his character's namesake but since there is no mention of Count Dracula impaling thousands of people on wooden poles, it's clear that "Dracula" is "Vlad the Impaler" in name only.

Stoker's inspiration for his vampire came from another source entirely. While touring the United States as the manager of famed British actor Henry Irving, Stoker was hard at work writing and researching his book. As he reached a section of the book that dealt with the final death of the vampire Lucy Westerna, he discovered a newspaper clipping about a strange ritual that occurred in Rhode Island concerning the grave of a young woman named Mercy Brown. He used the story as a basis for the fictional vampire hunter's destruction of Lucy.

Here's the scene that Stoker wrote for the book after reading the news clipping about the exhumation of Mercy Brown:

Arthur took the stake and the hammer, and when once his mind was set on action his hands never trembled nor even quivered. Van Helsing opened his missal and began to read, and Quincey and I followed as well as we could. Arthur placed the point over the heart, and as I looked, I could see its dint in the white flesh. Then he struck with all his might.

The thing in the coffin writhed, and a hideous, bloodcurdling screech came from the opened red lips. The body shook and quivered and twisted in wild contortions. The sharp white champed together till the lips were cut, and the mouth was smeared with a crimson foam. But Arthur never faltered. He looked like a figure of Thor as his untrembling arm rose and fell, driving deeper and deeper the mercy-bearing stake, whilst the blood from the pierced heart welled and spurted up around it. His face was set, and high duty seemed to shine through it. The sight of it gave us courage so that our voices seemed to ring through the little vault.

Stoker's book, *Dracula*, set the stage for every novel or story about vampires the followed it. The book has a unique place in history - it changed the folklore that already existed about what vampires could and couldn't do. Stoker took real folk legends and mixed them with elements from his own imagination and created a new popular conception about what a vampire should be. Folklore had inspired fiction, which, in turn, changed folklore.

A set of rules and attributes were born, although they were often altered by new books that came along and, later, by Hollywood movies.

Vampires were the "undead." They were lean, cadaverous, gaunt, thin, and sometimes skeletal like a long-dead corpse. They had red lips and long canine teeth. Their skin was white, almost transparent, and their flesh was always cold -- raised only to warmth after a particularly hearty meal of fresh blood. Their fingernails were curved like claws, their ears might be pointed, and their breath had the fetid, coppery smell of blood. They were also supernaturally strong, said to have the strength of a dozen or more men.

The vampire, as a living corpse, was permanently attached to its burial

place, or at least to the soil in which he had been buried. One of the many rules that seemed to govern a vampire's behavior was his need to return to his coffin, grave, or tomb before daylight each morning and sleep in it during the day. Although Hollywood suggested that sunlight could destroy a vampire, folklore said nothing of the kind, only relegated most of the vampire's activities to the nocturnal hours. Since they only prowled at night, Bram Stoker created the idea that a vampire must spend his days in his own coffin, very much at the mercy of the living vampire hunters.

Luckily, the vampire's weaknesses were overshadowed by its variety of magical powers -- not the least of which was his ability, in many tales, to get in and out of a grave through six feet of soil. Hungarian tales got around this problem by giving the vampire the supernatural ability to change into a cloud or mist. Stoker also used this trick in *Dracula* along with the Balkan belief that vampires can control a variety of fearsome animals like wolves or bats.

Occasionally, a few tales would give the vampire himself the ability to change into an animal. Occasionally, a vampire would become a wolf, a cat, or an owl, but only in a few Rumanian stories was it even vaguely mentioned that he could turn himself into a bat. Bats, of course, are nocturnal animals, often associated with dark and evil deeds, so it's not a surprise that it was worked into the vampire legend. But mention of this remained rare until the nineteenth century. It was at this time that European travelers first began to regularly visit South America -- and returned with tales about a bat that nourished itself solely and exclusively on blood. It was promptly named after its human counterpart from folklore and was just as promptly incorporated into the vampire stories.

Finally, one of the more useful of the vampire's talents was his hypnotic ability, which enabled him to mesmerize his victims and send them to sleep, so that he could feed on them without a struggle. A victim might wake up feeling tired and drained but would remember nothing of the previous night's visitor -- perhaps until he or she saw the two small punctures on the side of their neck.

Vampires also had many ways to recruit new bloodsuckers to the ranks. In the most traditional sense, a person could become a vampire after being fed upon and then drinking some of the vampire's own blood. This exchange of fluids seemed to be the most reliable method, although some stories claimed that a person who was drained of his blood would rise from the grave after three days as a vampire himself.

But according to the lore, this was, by no means, the only way that you might end up as one of the undead. The old tales stressed most frequently that anyone who died in a state of sin, without the blessings of the Church, risked becoming a vampire, as did those who were exceedingly wicked, or who dabbled in black magic.

But a man could turn into a vampire through no fault of his own. If his corpse did not receive full funeral rites of the Church, if he died without being baptized, or was murdered and his death was never avenged, he might become a vampire. Some were cursed, it was said, by something as simple as a cat jumping over a coffin that had not been buried. If anyone saw the cat perform this act, the transformation of a corpse into a vampire could be prevented with a little homemade magic. They simply had to place a piece of iron in the corpse's hand, put a piece of hawthorn in the coffin or hang a wreath of garlic around the cadaver's neck.

Such remedies were expected to protect a person from a vampire, as well. As the power of the Church swelled in Europe, Christian traditions began to mix with the folklore. The most common Christian element was the protective nature of the crucifix, which was believed to repel a vampire. Other Christian items could also be used, including holy water, relics, and communion wafers. Given the creature's evil nature, the best defense was reportedly the crucifix, which was regarded as the most powerful symbol of good. Wearing a cross around one's neck was always a good insurance policy, as was clutching a piece of silver, which was universally feared by every kind of evil spirit. As was running water, which had long been considered a barrier against evil spirits, too.

If vampire activity broke out in some region and no one knew where to find the monster, graves would be checked in the local cemetery. Each had to be opened and the corpses examined to find the one that had not decomposed. Such activity had to take place in the daylight when the vampire was dormant and could do no harm.

If a vampire were found at night, he could only be killed by a silver bullet that had been blessed by a priest. However, most vampire hunters considered it safer to hunt for their prey during the daylight hours. Once the body was disinterred, a wooden stake -- preferably of hawthorn, aspen or another sacred wood -- was driven through the creature's heart. Usually, this was the end of the ritual, but some traditions called for the vampire's head to be cut off, the body burned, or the heart torn from its body.

In America, our colonial ancestors were well aware of vampires, but they certainly did not see them as graceful "creatures of the night." The vampire was a death-bringer and something to be feared. An unsuspecting community that fell under the spell of one of these monsters could very well be destroyed. You see, in historic America, vampires were not mythical creatures from books and folklore, they were unquestionably real.

The stories of vampires in America originated in colonial New England. The influx of various immigrants from Europe -- British, Dutch, German, Romanian and Polish -- brought many old traditions to the American shores and created a place where many different beliefs could flourish, develop, and change. The German and Dutch settlers came to the New World with a number of supernatural creatures that amounted to the undead being called back to life. Nearly all of them attacked the living and drank their blood. Such ghoulish traditions blended with Native American myths of nameless creatures that were halfway between some sort of monster and a ghost. Both the Wampanoag of Massachusetts and the Narragansett of Rhode Island told of a thing that had the form of a man but hid in the shadows of the forest. It would attack hunters and travelers unlucky enough to pass by. No weapon could kill it and a man had only to speak its name to summon it from the dark woods. Exactly what this creature did with its victims was unknown, but it was unwise to cross its path. It's easy to see how belief in such a being could easily mix with some of the mythology brought to America by the new settlers.

Another element in the American vampire mythology was religion. The stern Christianity of the Puritans shaped and moldered the lives of New England settlers and the Devil was everywhere in those days. Their only protection from diabolical attacks was their faith and belief in God. From the earliest days of the Pilgrims in 1620, the colonies framed their world through religion and supernatural intervention.

In the 1740s, a radical minster named George Whitefield traveled along the American coast, preaching to crowds who gathered to hear him at the start of what came to be called the First Great Awakening. From this period emerged groups with radical theories regarding salvation, sin, and faith. Cults and sects sprang up everywhere and offshoots of new religions from older ones came and went. Many of their beliefs were strange - then and now. The followers of a minister named Robert Browne, for example, claimed that the Devil was a woman and, consequently, no woman could enter heaven. Saintly women were turned into men at the time of death.

Mother Anne Lee's Shakers, who had fled England in 1774, believed that lust was the Original Sin, so any contact between men and women was forbidden.

A Perfectionist named Shadrack Ireland believed that the "second coming" of Christ was imminent and he instructed his followers to place themselves on stone slabs in sealed underground chambers beneath the Massachusetts hills. That way, when the Trumpet of God sounded, their bodies would be whole and intact.

For many of the faithful, sin and evil - and the avoidance of both - became serious preoccupations. Once a man had given his life to God, the Devil would stop at nothing to destroy him. The Devil's agents were everywhere. The Native Americans were often described in the writings of ministers of the era as "worshippers of the Devil." When they attacked the white settlements, it was unquestionably the work of Satan. And God permitted

Many new cults and sects appeared during America's First Great Awakening, which would lead to many radical beliefs - including in vampires.

these atrocities to occur because of the sins of the colonists, whether real or imagined. Such raids were punishment for the colonists and a powerful reminder of the evil that lurked in the shadowy corners of the new land.

On May 19, 1780, a spectacular event occurred that shook New England to its core and galvanized many of the radical churches. It was already a time of religious fervor as itinerant preachers traveled among the people, preaching of sin and the presence of evil. Then, at mid-day on May 19, the sky suddenly went dark, and the sun disappeared. The sky was darker than even the blackest night, forcing lamps and candles to be lit. What caused the famous "New England's Dark Day" is unknown. It may have been a solar eclipse, heavy cloud cover, thick fog, or even the smoke from forest fires. The total darkness extended as far as

Barnstable, Massachusetts and was even experienced in Pennsylvania and New Jersey. While undoubtedly some sort of strange, natural phenomenon, the religious felt there could only be one explanation -- the end of the world was coming. The darkness lasted until about midnight and when it finally dispersed, the stars could be seen shining above. The world had not come to an end.

The effect of the "Dark Day" on New England's religious community, however, was electric. If the darkness was not a sign of Christ's return, then it had to be something else, perhaps even more dire. Many said that it was a warning from God that America was a place of sin. It was a hint of things to come if men did not mend their ways and follow the word of the Lord.

But, keep in mind, just about everything was treated as a sign from God or evidence of the Devil's work in those days. The Devil was stepping up his efforts to bring ruin and damnation to America and, as if to prove it, many local villages and towns experienced epidemics of typhoid fever and smallpox in the months that followed.

Fear, myths, rumors, and religion all combined to create the legends of American vampires, but the greatest element in all of this was disease.

The conditions in which many of the settlers lived were poor and unsanitary. Many of them lived on the edges of lakes, bogs, and swamps, which were perfect breeding grounds for all sorts of ailments, most of them fatal. Epidemics of various kinds swept through the colonies, claiming the lives of the weak and vulnerable as they passed. Once again, given the religious fervor of the time, epidemics were regarded as another sign of God's judgment upon a sinful people. Because of the wet, unclean conditions and poor sanitation, typhoid, tuberculosis, and many other forms of respiratory and lung infections, flourished through the colonies. It was not uncommon for entire families to sometimes be lost to a single epidemic.

One of the first writers to connect the stories of vampires with epidemics was an anthropologist named George R. Stetson. He wrote an article called "The Animistic Vampire of New England" for the *American Anthropologist* journal in January 1896. He wrote of many places in New England where, thanks to isolation and poverty, a belief in vampires still flourished. He made a connection between the epidemics of yesterday and the belief that vampires preyed on the families of various regions.

Between about 1780 and the latter part of the 1800s, plagues of typhoid, smallpox, and consumption - what tuberculosis was called at the time - killed large numbers of people in communities that had already been devastated by poverty and a decline in the farming that once been the lifeblood of the town. Poor diet and harsh life often took their toll on the more vulnerable, making them easy victims for all sorts of contagions. Perhaps looking for some sort of explanation for the lives that were ruined, vampires were blamed. In Stetson's writings, he mentioned a curious custom that occurred after certain epidemics. Bodies of victims were apparently exhumed and examined, and, in many cases, hearts and some internal organs were burned in an effort to prevent the corpse from coming back to claim the lives of other members of his or her family.

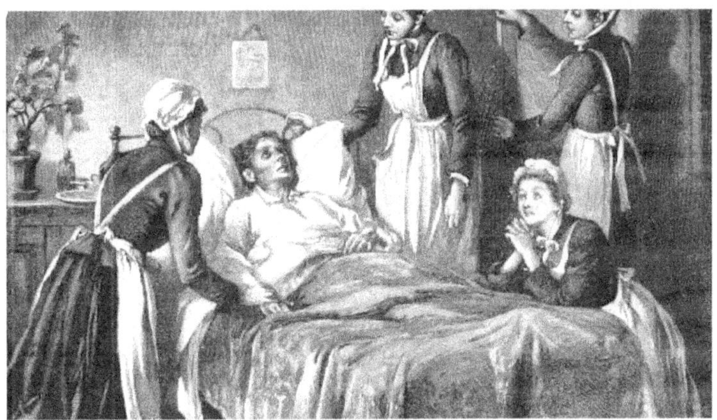

Consumption victims of the nineteenth century were often believed to also be the victims of vampires.

How did this connection get started? Historically speaking, it's not hard to understand how consumption came to be associated with vampires. It was the great plague of the nineteenth century. Across America, the death tolls were staggering. The illness was spread by everyday living conditions -- large families, often poorly nourished, who shared living space for long periods of time. It was quite normal for the disease to run through families. Highly contagious and generally fatal, tuberculosis was so lethal that doctors called it the first disease "to deter practitioners from attempting a cure."

As consumption claimed life after life, it began to be called the "White Death," which spoke volumes about how it affected its victims. As the disease progressed, the body was transformed from its previous ruddy complexion to the skin becoming stark white, almost ghostly and translucently thin. A network of light blue veins became visible beneath the surface. Victims often ran fevers, which caused their cheeks to become reddened; they had difficulty breathing and developed a terrible cough that often brought up bloody phlegm. They suffered from fainting spells, anemia, weight loss, and an increasingly fragile demeanor. The thin, pale, weak, and listless victims often came to resemble a living cadaver. Oddly, due to certain romantic and beauty standards of the time, these symptoms made the victims, especially young women, strangely alluring. As the illness progressed, they became more beautiful, it was believed, while their bodies, health, and strength were consumed by the incurable disease.

It was probably easy for early New Englanders to imagine this wasting away -- the process of being consumed by the disease -- as the result of a vampire preying on the very life of the victim. No doubt, to some, the resulting mysteriously heightened feminine beauty was evidence of a transformation from victim to vampire. A seemingly bizarre component of the disease contributed to the illusion -- consumptives occasionally experienced surprising periods of manic energy. Many were known to have powerful sex drives. Some have suggested that these attributes proved that the individuals were clinging to life in a manner that could survive the grave.

At some point in New England history, it came to be accepted that when someone died of consumption, they could come back from the dead and drain the life from their surviving relatives. To stop this, family members would open their grave and attempt to kill them again. When relatives opened the coffins of the recently deceased consumptives, the corpses, formerly thin and frail, were often found to be bloated and engorged. Fingernails seemed to have grown into claws and, perhaps the most damning evidence, blood was often found in the mouth. There were even some accounts of bodies jerking and gurgling as the remains were being mutilated. Of course, all of this "evidence" of vampirism could be explained scientifically in these modern times. The decomposition of the body caused it to bloat; the flesh receded from the fingers, making the nails look as though they had grown; loss of tissue in the lungs from the disease caused blood to remain in the mouth, etc. At that time, however, those who went looking did not have to search very far to find "proof" that the dead had returned as a vampire.

Driving a wooden stake through the heart of the vampire was a European tradition and was not practiced by New Englanders. Instead, they removed the monster's heart and burned it. Decapitation was also popular, as were other mutilations of the body. In each case, disturbing the body seemed to bring the trouble to an end -- and it kept the dead from leaving the grave.

America's historical record is filled with many strange things, from stories of ghosts and monsters to unexplained lights, mythical creatures - and vampires.

One of the earliest stories of a vampire in New England was recorded in Manchester, Vermont, and dates back to the late eighteenth century. The account was discovered in the personal papers of Judge John S. Pettibone and was written down at some point between 1857 and 1872. As far as could be discovered, the story is true.

The events began on March 8, 1789 when Captain Isaac Burton married a beautiful young woman named Rachel Harris. She was from a prominent family in the region and the marriage was praised in the Manchester community. The captain seemed to have found the perfect partner, but unfortunately the marriage did not last long. Shortly after the wedding, Rachel's health began to fail. Consumption was prevalent in the area and Rachel succumbed to it, dying slowly and painfully. During her illness, she coughed up large quantities of blood, her skin became pale, and she went into a severe decline. Less than one year after she married Isaac Burton, she died on February 1, 1790.

Captain Burton was distraught over the death of his young wife and he mourned her for many months. After nearly a year had passed, he decided to marry again. He took a new bride, Hulda Powell, daughter of a wealthy landowner, on January 4, 1791. Hulda was described as a lovely, fit, and healthy young woman - but her health soon failed. A few months into the marriage, Hulda also began to display symptoms of the same wasting disease that had taken Rachel. Her vitality faded away, she became unnaturally pale, and she developed a harsh, bloody cough. Desperate to save his second wife from death, Burton spent huge sums of money on her treatment, bringing in physicians from large cities to investigate his wife's condition. Although they offered opinions and prescribed tonics for the declining woman, they were of little use and soon Hulda was confined to her bed, just as Rachel had been. The stories say that she became delusional in her illness, claiming that she saw Rachel in her room, her mouth covered in blood and smelling of dirt. The stories frightened Burton and his wife's family and they took turns staying with her at night, looking after her, and perhaps protecting her from her delusions. As time passed, Hulda continued to deteriorate.

One of the relatives who sat beside Hulda's bed was an elderly aunt that was well-versed in the folklore of the region. She listened to her niece's tales of late-night visitations from a ghastly-looking Rachel Harris and soon talk turned to vampires. She offered Isaac a rather chilling explanation for what was ailing his sickly wife. Bluntly, she told him that she believed a wraith of sorts was draining the life from Hulda's body. The only way to stop it was to remove the body of Rachel from her grave and burn it. After that, Hulda had a chance to recover but, even then, recovery was not certain. But it was certain that if nothing were done at all, Hulda would surely die -- and soon the vampire would perhaps prey on other members of the family.

Frightened and at a loss, Burton approached an old friend and town selectman named Timothy Mead to request an exhumation of Rachel's body. Mead refused, telling his friend that vampires were only an old superstition. Rachel had been a respectable young woman from an upstanding family, and she didn't deserve to be connected to such nonsense. The matter was put aside, but Hulda grew weaker with each passing day. The old aunt's beliefs seemed to be supported by her decline, especially after Hulda began to complain of feeling a pressing weight on her chest at night, as though someone was sitting on it. In addition, she now had flecks of blood around the sides of her mouth, as if someone had been taking it from her body. Burton and several relatives remained by the young woman's bed each night, only to be startled from sleep by Hulda's cries and screams that Rachel was in the room with her. They never saw anything, but Hulda was clearly terrified.

Rumors began to spread around town about vampires, but could there by any truth to them? Hulda's suffering could easily be explained as the symptoms of consumption, but to Captain Burton and many of the people in Manchester, the symptoms only meant one thing -- a vampire was at work.

Burton approached Timothy Mead again and this time, aware of the rising tide of rumor and fear in town, he arranged for an exhumation. On a February morning in 1793, Rachel's body was removed from the cemetery and taken to the shop of the local blacksmith. In spite of their fear, a large number of people gathered to watch the events. The casket, once opened, revealed a bloated corpse that was scarcely recognizable as the young and beautiful Rachel Harris. Around her mouth were the dark stains of blood, which were noticed immediately by the crowd. Whispers spread that the corpse was so bloated because it was engorged with blood. This seemed to be incontrovertible evidence that Rachel was indeed a vampire.

Her heart, lungs, and liver were removed and were cast into the searing heat of the blacksmith's forge. According to the account, a foul stench came from the burning organs and several onlookers later declared that they heard the sigh of a woman as the black smoke curled up into the sky. Others claimed they saw what looked like a black serpent slither upward in the smoke and vanish as it began to disperse.

If Isaac Burton expected his wife to recover after the gruesome task at the blacksmith shop, he was extremely disappointed. Although she did rally briefly, Hulda was too weakened by her illness and did not survive. She died on September 6, 1793, and despite some initial fears that she might return from the grave as Rachel did; nothing more was heard from her.

Isaac Burton continued to live in Manchester and married two more times during his life - but he certainly never forgot his first one.

The story of Rachel Harris Burton, the wife who returned from the grave to prey on her successor, spread wildly throughout New England. It reinforced old beliefs, not only about vampires but about the presence of evil in the land and about the necessity of living a good and proper life.

Within three years of the exhumation of Rachel Burton, another vampire account reared its ugly head in New England. This tale centered around Cumberland, Rhode Island and the death of a young woman named Abigail Staples, who died near the end of 1793 at the age of only 23. It was believed that she died from consumption, but unfortunately, that was not the last her family saw of her - or so the story goes.

On February 8, 1796, Abigail's father, a prosperous merchant named Stephen Staples, approached the Cumberland town council with an unusual request -- he wanted to dig up the body of his dead daughter. In what he described as an "experiment," he wished to dig up the body of Abigail, who had died several months before, to see if an exhumation might save the life of his other daughter, Lavinia. Abigail had been a moody, unhappy girl who, while never married, often dreamed of a husband and children. When her sister married a young man

BELIEVE IN VAMPIRES.

Rhode Islanders Who Are Sure That They Do Exist.

Instances Told of Where the Living Have Been Attacked and Preyed Upon by These Representatives of an Unseen World.

A MEMBER OF THE ANTI-VAMPIRE PARTY.

named Stephen Chace, it was believed that Abigail harbored a deep resentment toward the marriage. Her own dreams of matrimony were cut short by consumption and she died.

Shortly after her sister's death, Lavinia began to exhibit symptoms like those Abigail had suffered from and her health began to deteriorate. She was confined to her bed for a time and as she slept, she had visions of a dark figure crouched at the end of her bed. It jumped onto her chest, crushing her with its weight and stealing the breath from her body. Her family assumed that the dreams would pass with the sickness but then one morning, her husband was very disturbed when she sat upright in bed and uttered the single word -- "Abigail."

Stephen was troubled by this and went to see his father-in-law. Stephen Staples listened to what the young man said. He knew the legends of vampires but had never put much faith in the stories.

However, the incident occurred at an interesting time. There were several people in the area who were also suffering from tuberculosis and, in keeping with the religious fervor of the times, several local ministers had proclaimed that the illness was God's punishment on his wayward people. The Devil was near, the preachers claimed, and would soon make his presence known. Staples was a man who took his faith seriously and so he decided to take his son-in-law's concerns to the authorities.

The members of the town council reacted with skepticism. While they were sympathetic toward the grieving father, they believed that vampires belonged in the realm of folklore and ignorant superstition. However, they were also acutely aware of the sermons being given by ministers in the area and how they had stirred up notions of ever-present devils and demons. Sensing their uncertainty about how to proceed, Staples pressed the issue, saying that if the Devil was close at hand, then demon vampires might be among them, as well. Stephen Chace then made his own impassioned plea,

suggesting that it would be for the good of the community to dispel the terror that gripped so many people. Abigail's corpse should be exhumed and inspected and, if nothing were amiss, the girl would be reburied with decency. Somewhat reluctantly, the council authorized the exhumation. They only had one stipulation -- the "experiment" had to be kept as secret as possible and no written record of it could be kept.

In keeping with the council's request, Staples, Chace and three hired men went out to a small graveyard on the Staples' property. They arrived after nightfall, lanterns in hand, and unearthed Abigail's body. No record exists about what they found but local legend recalls that whatever young Stephen Chace saw when the coffin was opened that night almost drove him mad. He wandered the countryside, muttering to himself until sunrise. Stephen never again spoke of that night or what he had witnessed, but he was a changed man after that. For the rest of his life, he was troubled by horrible nightmares. Legend also claims that one of the workmen who unearthed the coffin committed suicide a short time later.

What became of Lavinia Chace is unknown. She simply vanished from history after that. She might have recovered, or she, too, might have perished from consumption. There is no marker to identify her grave to say when or how she died, and no mention is made of her in any subsequent account.

There is no record of any similar occurrences in the region, and it is unclear if any similar deaths took place in the wake of Abigail's demise. However, there is a curious headstone that was erected nearby for a man named Simon Whipple Aldrich. It can be found in the Union Cemetery Annex and it bears a very odd inscription: "Although consumption's vampire grasp had seized thy mortal frame."

Simon Aldrich was the youngest son of Colonel Dexter Aldrich and his wife, Margery. He died on May 6, 1841, presumably of tuberculosis. However, the strange mention of the word vampire in the inscription has intrigued historians over the years. Why was it included on the headstone? It may, of course, be only a turn of phrase, but it may also be a reminder of the dark days of Abigail Staples -- and perhaps a part of the indelible mark that she left on the history of the community.

The next vampire tale has traditionally always started with a dream.

Stutley Tillinghast was a prosperous apple farmer from Exeter, Rhode Island. He was liked and admired in the community and was active in the local church. He was a good provider, probably everyone in town agreed, and he was an excellent father. He and his wife, Honor, were parents to 14 children and all of them, against the odds in those days, had survived into early adulthood.

Then one night, the farmer awoke after an unsettling and disturbing dream. The nightmare was especially vivid and had left him in a cold sweat. He dreamed that he was walking between the rows of his apple orchard. On one side, the trees were extremely healthy, their limbs weighted down by an abundance of fruit. On the other side of the orchard, the trees had withered and died. The branches had dropped their leaves and wasted and rotted apples lay scattered about on the ground. Somewhere, in the dark shadows of the dream orchard, he heard the voice of his daughter Sarah calling to him. As he turned to see where she was, a cold wind blew through the trees and chilled him to the bone. Branches creaked in the trees and leaves swirled about his feet, scraping and rustling as they passed. The voice faded and as it did, the stench of decay spread from the diseased side of the orchard and he knew that half of his crop had been lost. Tillinghast awoke with a terrible feeling of dread. He was sure the dream was some sort of portent of things to come --but of what?

Fearing that the dream predicted something terrible about the coming season's apple harvest, the farmer was greatly relieved when it was successful as always. The unsettling vision remained with him for a while longer, but then his fear began to fade as the family settled in for the winter.

A short time later, Sarah, the couple's oldest daughter, grew sick. Sarah had always been a moody young woman, preferring to stay in her room and read and wander alone to a nearby graveyard instead of spending time with the rest of the family. At first, no one noticed when she began to skip meals or stay in bed a little longer than usual. But as she became weaker and her skin grew pale and sickly, her mother realized that she was very ill. At the end of 1799, she died. The cause was, of course, given as "consumption," and she was laid to rest in the family plot, a short distance from the Tillinghast house.

But, in time, stories would claim that she returned from the grave.

A few weeks after her death, the Tillinghast's youngest son, James, came down to breakfast one morning looking pale and shaken. He claimed that his chest hurt badly, "where Sarah touched him." His mother assured him that it had only been a bad dream and yet she could hear an unhealthy rattle in his lungs. He was sent back to bed and extra blankets were added to keep him warm. In the nights that followed,

The Tillinghast family burial ground - was one of them a vampire? The people of Exeter believed it to be true.

he continued to claim that Sarah came to visit him in the night and would often touch him. As he grew sicker, his parents assumed that his stories were the result of his fevers, but they did not ponder the meaning of them for long. James soon followed his sister to the grave.

A short time later, James' sister, Andris, grew sick. Her sister, Ruth, also began wasting away.

Both died and it seemed that an unknown blight was now facing the family. Before the girls died, they began to complain repeatedly about their dead sister, Sarah, and claimed that she was coming to them in the night. She came as a ghostly figure, entering the room through the window. Sarah would then come to the side of the bed and push down on each girl's chest, making it difficult for her to breathe.

EXHUMED THE BODIES.

Testing a Horrible Superstition in the Town of Exeter.

In the days and weeks that followed, more of the Tillinghast children weakened and died. The fifth child, Hannah, was married and lived several miles away with her husband. She often visited her parents and helped Honor with the daily chores. On several nights, though, after leaving the Tillinghast farm, she was convinced that she was being followed. One night, she caught a glimpse of someone in the shadows and thought it was her sister, Sarah -- but Sarah was dead. Oddly, she had dreams that night that Sarah was in her bedroom with her. A short time later, Hannah grew sick and began wasting away. She died in the late spring of 1800.

By the time Hannah died, Stutley Tillinghast began to recall the strange dream that he had experienced about the apple orchard. In this vision, exactly half of the orchard had withered and died. He finally realized what the dream had been trying to tell him. In despair, he realized that seven of his children were going to die. He didn't try to ponder the supernatural meanings behind the dream, however. At this point, he was trying to puzzle out the meaning behind his children's complaints about nighttime visits from Sarah. Before each of them died, they claimed the girl came into their room at night. What could this mean?

Another death followed and then the seventh Tillinghast child, Ezra, also began to complain of strange feelings of fatigue and of seeing Sarah in his room at night. He also succumbed to the mysterious consumption. Soon after, Honor also began to weaken. She began to dream of Sarah coming to her in the darkness, as well.

After talking it over with some of his neighbors, Tillinghast began to believe that Sarah was responsible for the string of deaths in his family. Knowing the only way to stop the deaths was to take action, Stutley, along with two of his hired men, made his way to the cemetery where the body of Sarah had been buried. They took along shovels, ropes, and a flask of oil.

Throughout the night, the men worked at digging up the coffins of all the Tillinghast children. All of them had been in the earth for more than six months when the caskets were opened; they found the bodies to be rotting and decayed -- except for one. Sarah's body, it was said, was in perfect condition. She was lying as if in repose. Her hair and nails had grown, her flesh was soft and supple, and her eyes were open, staring up into the sky. When the coffin was removed and one of the workmen looked down on her face, he immediately fell to his knees and began to pray.

When he saw his daughter, Stutley was seized with horror and he rushed to the wagon and returned with the can of oil. Taking a large knife from his belt, he bent down into the coffin and slashed open Sarah's chest. Her heart and liver were cut out and Tillinghast doused them with oil and set them on fire. As they burned, a sharp stench filled the air and the men watched as the smoke curled into the air above the burial ground. The organs turned to ash and the men, still shaking, judged that the danger was past. They reinterred all the coffins and left the cemetery as the sun began to rise.

Thanks to her husband's daring act, Honor soon recovered her health and later bore her husband two more children. All the remaining children outlived their parents.

Stutley Tillinghast's eerie dream had come true - half of his life's crop had perished from an unexplainable scourge, but the other half had survived.

The story of America's last vampire, Mercy Brown, is a shadow that still lingers over Rhode Island today. Even though it came to a cruel and bloody end in 1892, the tale had its beginnings years before, in 1883, when consumption was claiming lives in the area around Exeter.

George Brown was a hard-working farmer who prospered in this part of southern Rhode Island, not far from Providence. He and his wife, Mary Eliza, had raised six children and lived a comfortable, but simple life.

But in late 1883, the first in a series of terrible events occurred on the Brown farm when Mary Eliza began to show the telltale signs of having contracted consumption. The sturdy, once healthy woman began to suffer from fainting spells and periods of weakness. Most of all, she was gripped with a harsh cough that kept her awake through the night. After these horrible fits of coughing, the handkerchief that she kept pressed to her mouth would be covered in blood. The disease began to ravage her body

The temporary receiving vault at Chestnut Hill Cemetery, where Mercy Brown was placed in January 1892. It was to be used until the ground thawed enough to allow her body to be buried.

and on December 8, she slipped into unconsciousness and did not awaken. She died at the age of only 36.

Seven months later, the Browns' oldest daughter, 20-year-old Mary Olive, also came down with the dreaded illness. She developed the now familiar symptoms of weight loss, weakness, and a wracking cough. Mary Olive grew paler and weaker with each passing day and on June 6, 1884; she followed her mother to the grave.

Several years of peace followed the death of Mary Olive and during this time, Edwin Brown, George's only son, got married and bought his own farm in nearby West Wickford. He hoped to make a life for himself and his new bride while he worked in a store to support his family and save money for the future.

Their life was a happy one until 1891, when Edwin began to notice the symptoms of the disease that had killed his sister and mother. He resigned from his job and, following advice from friends, moved west to Colorado Springs. The city had begun to develop a reputation for helping to ease the suffering of consumption patients and Edwin hoped the local mineral waters and the drier climate might restore his health.

While Edwin and his wife were out west, things took a darker turn for the Brown family in Exeter. In January 1892, Edwin received word that his 19-year-old sister, Mercy Lena, had also become sick and died. Her consumption was diagnosed as the "galloping" variety and she quickly passed away and was entombed in the receiving vault at Chestnut Hill Cemetery.

Edwin realized that his own health was not improving in Colorado. Together, he and his wife decided that they should return home so that Edwin could spend the remainder of his days with family, friends, and loved ones. They made the journey back to Rhode Island and moved in with Edwin's in-laws, Mr. and Mrs. Willet Himes.

By the time Edwin returned to Rhode Island, his father was in a dreadful and worried state. Friends were convinced that the family was being preyed on by a vampire and suggested that Brown should exhume the bodies of the other family members and see which one of them it was. While upset and worried, he refused to go along with such nonsense. It was superstitious fear, and he would not be a party to it.

But one of Brown's younger friends -- his identity has never been documented -- took matters into his own hands. He decided to pay a visit to Dr. Harold Metcalf, who was not only the district medical examiner but was also the physician who had treated Mercy Brown during her illness. He asked Metcalf for his help. He explained that Edwin was also suffering from the same disease and that several friends and neighbors believed that the only way in which his life could be saved was to have the bodies of the mother and two daughters exhumed in order to ascertain if the heart of any of the bodies still contained blood. If any of them did, then that dead body was feeding off the living tissue and blood of Edwin. Metcalf considered this as absurd as George Brown did and sent the young man away.

At some point over the course of the next week, George Brown's friends finally convinced him of the possibility that one of the dead women was indeed a vampire. Perhaps, only because he had exhausted all other options, Brown agreed to the exhumation - but only if Dr. Metcalf would also attend. The young man who had previously gone to see the doctor returned to his door once again. He told him that George Brown, though not believing in the superstition himself, wanted to pacify his friends by allowing the graves to be opened. Because of this, he asked Dr. Metcalf if he would attend and perform the autopsies. Dr. Metcalf again balked at the idea, but eventually agreed to go along; realizing that he could not persuade them from what they believed was their duty.

By the time Metcalf arrived at the cemetery, the bodies of Mary Brown and her daughter, Mary Olive, had already been unearthed. Mary had been in the ground almost nine years at this point and she was in an advanced state of decay. Some of her muscles and flesh existed in a mummified state, but there were no signs of blood in her heart. The men then opened the coffin of Mary Olive, who had also died years before. According to a newspaper account, only a skeleton and a thick growth of hair remained. Dr. Metcalf stated with certainty that they were, "just what might be expected from a similar examination of almost any person after the same length of time."

Mercy's body had not yet been buried. She had died in the winter when the ground was too hard for a burial. Her body had rested for the past two months inside a small crypt on the cemetery grounds. The coffin was placed on a small cart inside the tomb. Once the casket was opened, Dr. Metcalf looked inside and began a quick autopsy of the corpse. He noted some signs of decay and the marks left by consumption on her lungs. This did not convince him that she was a vampire, so he finished his examination and announced his findings to the men who had gathered to see to the gruesome tasks at hand. Metcalf told them that there was nothing amiss with the body, but they didn't see things the same way that he did. When he was unable to convince them, he left the cemetery.

To the other men - and perhaps even to Edwin, who was present for the exhumations -- Mercy seemed relatively intact, or at least more so than she should be after being dead for two months. In addition, they were also sure that her body had moved. She had been laid to rest on her back and somehow the corpse was now resting on its side. Could she have left the casket? Dr. Metcalf, they believed, was simply trying to protect his reputation as a man of science and wanted no part of vampires.

The men were suspicious that something was wrong with Mercy Brown and what happened next convinced them entirely. One of the men opened her heart with his knife and was startled to see fresh blood come pouring out of the organ. It was quickly removed from her chest. They also cut out her liver because, even though it contained no fresh blood, it was in a remarkably preserved state. The organs were burned on the stone cemetery wall and the men watched as they were engulfed by flames. Once it had burned, the ashes were gathered with which to make a tonic that would hopefully cure Edwin of the disease.

Edwin consumed the macabre mixture, but it did him little good. On May 2, he joined his mother and sisters in death and was buried at Chestnut Hill. While his death was tragic, all was not lost. He became the last of the Brown family to die from consumption -- or from the ravages of a vampire, depending on what you believe.

The exhumations, autopsies, and burnings that were designed to save the living of New England from being consumed by the dead ended with Mercy Brown. The germs that caused tuberculosis had been discovered in

The grave of Mercy Brown - America's Last Vampire

seemed more focused on pointing out the superstitious ignorance of country folk than in studying the effects the old folklore had on the lives and deaths of the people involved. Mercy was finally placed in her grave soon after the incident took place -- but that was not the end of her story.

Mercy Brown lived on, not only in Rhode Island legend, but in other ways, as well.

1882 and the fact that the disease was contagious was established not long afterward. The discovery dismissed the superstitious belief that the illness was caused by vampires that fed on the living, but news of such discoveries was slow in arriving to places like rural New England. Even if the Brown family and their friends heard such accounts, the claim that consumption was caused by invisible organisms that were passed from one person to another would have seemed perhaps even more unlikely than the idea that people weakened and died after being preyed upon by the dead.

The accounts of the Mercy Brown exhumation had a brief life in the newspapers of the day, all of which

Author H.P. Lovecraft wrote a horror story called "The Shunned House" in 1924 and it was first published in the October 1937 issue of *Weird Tales* magazine. While not the primary focus of the story, the 1892 exhumation does manage to be mentioned when Lovecraft refers to the Exeter "rustics" and even names one of the characters in the story Mercy. Lovecraft relished New England folklore and legends and incorporated many of them into his stories.

A more important appearance of Mercy Brown in literature occurred in 1897 when the story of her exhumation was used in an altered form for Bram Stoker's novel, *Dracula*. When Stoker passed away, his years of collected articles and book materials were sold. Among them was the material that he used to research his groundbreaking vampire novel, including clippings about the exhumation of Mercy Brown.

When he altered the events and added characters to fit his story, it becomes obvious that Dr. Van Helsing and his group of vampire hunters are following a scenario much like the one that occurred in the town of Exeter -- earning Mercy Brown a place in vampire literature history.

To this day, Mercy Brown has not been forgotten by the people of Rhode Island. She retains a place of honor as the last American vampire, casting a very long shadow that stretches back to a time when vampires and consumption were both a part of everyday life. In the years that followed Mercy's death, tuberculosis claimed many more victims than America's "vampires" ever did. The end result for both the disease and the mythical cause was the same, though.

Both were conquered by science.

The belief in vampires faded as superstitions about them became a thing of the past. Tuberculosis turned out to be much harder to kill.

It was many years after Mercy Brown before effective treatments, medicines, and cures began to be developed to treat the illness. Millions

EXHUMED THE BODIES.

Testing a Horrible Superstition in the Town of Exeter.

BODIES OF DEAD RELATIVES TAKEN FROM THEIR GRAVES.

They Had All Died of Consumption, and the Belief Was That Live Flesh and Blood Would be Found That Fed Upon the Bodies of the Living.

Within a few years George T. Brown of Exeter has been bereft of a wife and two daughters by that dreaded disease consumption. His wife, Mary E., daughter of Pardon M. Arnold, was first stricken down about eight years ago, leaving her husband with six children, one son and five daughters. Within two years from the mother's death the eldest daughter, Olive B., died of the same disease, leaving the other members of the family apparently in good health. In a few years the son, Edwin A., who has been employed as clerk by G. T. Cranston and by Taylor & Davis of Lafayette, was taken ill, and by advice of friends went to Colorado Springs about 18 months ago. During his absence the past winter another daughter, Mercy Lena, who appeared in good health at his departure, passed away after a few months of suffering. Three weeks ago Edwin A., finding his health so rapidly failing, came back to Rhode Island and now is critically ill at the residence of Willet Himes, his father-in-law.

During the few weeks past Mr. Brown has been besieged on all sides by a number of people, who expressed implicit faith in the old theory that by some unexplained and unreasonable way in some part of the deceased relative's body live flesh and blood might be found, which is supposed to feed upon the living who are in feeble health. Mr. Brown, having no confidence in the old-time theory, and also getting no encouragement from the medical fraternity, did not yield to their importunities until Thursday afternoon, when an investigation was held under the direction of Harold Metcalf, M. D., of Wickford. The bodies of the wife and two daughters, who were buried in the Exeter Cemetery, were exhumed and an examination made, finding nothing but skeletons of the bodies of the wife and eldest daughter. After examination of the body of M. Lena, who was buried

more died before tuberculosis finally became -- just like the American vampire -- a thing of the past.

The
MORBID CURIOUS
Contributors NO. 3

AMANDA R. WOOMER

Writer, anthropologist, and former international English teacher, Amanda R. Woomer was born and raised in Buffalo, NY. A member of the Society for Psychical Research, she is a featured writer for the award-winning *Haunted Magazine* and the owner of Spook-Eats. She is the author of *A Haunted Atlas of Western New York*, *The Spirit Guide: America's Haunted Breweries, Distilleries, and Wineries*, and *The Ghosts of the Ghostlight Theatre* as well as two books in the *Creepy Books for Creepy Kids* series. She has also begun curating the all-new all-female paranormal journal, *The Feminine Macabre*. Follow her spooky adventures at spookeats.com and on Facebook, Instagram, and Twitter.

SYLVIA SHULTS

Sylvia Shults is the author of *44 Years in Darkness, Fractured Spirits: Hauntings at the Peoria State Hospital*, and other books of true ghost stories. She has spent the past twenty years working in a library, slowly smuggling words out in her pockets day by day to build a book of her own and she sits in dark, spooky, haunted places so you don't have to. After battling an intense, lifelong fear of the dark, Sylvia decided to become a ghost hunter. As a paranormal investigator, she has made many media appearances, including a tiny part in the Ghost Hunters episode "Prescription for Fear", about the Peoria State Hospital. She is a recurring guest on Ron Hood's podcast

Ron's Amazing Stories, with the monthly segment "Ghost Stories With Sylvia". She is also the writer, director, producer, and host of the true ghost story podcast Lights Out, available on YouTube, iTunes, iHeart Radio, Spotify, and anywhere else great podcasts are found. Sylvia loves hearing from her readers, especially when they have spooky stories of their own to share with her. She can be found at www.sylviashults.wordpress.com and on Facebook at the pages for Fractured Spirits and Ghosts of the Illinois River.

MICHELLE L. HAMILTON

Michelle L. Hamilton earned her MA in History from San Diego State University. Hamilton is the author or editor of several books including *"I Would Still Be Drowned in Tears": Spiritualism in Abraham Lincoln's White House* and *Mary Ball Washington: The Mother of George Washington.* Her latest book is *Civil War Ghosts* published by Haunted Road Media. A lifelong student of history, Hamilton has worked as a docent at several museums across the county. She is currently the manager of the Mary Washington House in Fredericksburg, VA. You can follow her at her blog Paranormal History at https://paranormalhist.blogspot.com/

TROY TAYLOR

Troy is an author of books on ghosts, hauntings, true crime, the unexplained, and the supernatural in America and the editor and creator of "The Morbid Curious." He is also the founder of American Hauntings Ink, which offers books, ghost tours, events, and weekend excursions. He was born and raised in the Midwest and currently divides his time between Illinois and the far-flung reaches of America.

Special Thanks To:

April Slaughter

Amanda Woomer

Sylvia Shults

Adam Seaman

Michelle Hamilton

Lisa Taylor and Lux

Kaylan Schardan

Cody Beck

Lois Taylor

Orrin Taylor

Rene Kruse

Rachael Horath

Elyse and Thomas Reihner

Bethany Horath

Becky Ray

John Winterbauer

Maggie and Packy Lundholm

Tom and Michelle Bonadurer

Susan Kelly and Amy Bouyear

Cheryl Stamp and Sheryel

Williams-Staab

American Hauntings Crew